AN ACTUARIAL MODEL FOR COSTING UNIVERSAL HEALTH COVERAGE IN ARMENIA

Rouselle F. Lavado, George Schieber, Ammar Aftab, Saro Tsaturyan, and Hiddo A. Huitzing

DECEMBER 2020

ASIAN DEVELOPMENT BANK

ADB

Notes:
In this publication, "$" refers to United States dollars.

On the cover: Ruins of the Zvartnos temple in Yerevan, Armenia, with mount Ararat
in the background (Alamy stock photo) and Republic Square of Yerevan (ADB photo).

Cover design by Josef Ilumin.

Printed on recycled paper

Contents

Appendixes

References — **102**

Tables and Figures

Tables

Figures

Acknowledgments

This report was prepared by a team led by Rouselle F. Lavado, senior health specialist; and composed of George Schieber, health financing consultant; Ammar Aftab, actuarial consultant; Saro Tsaturyan, health policy consultant; and Hiddo A. Huitzing, health specialist of the Social Sector Division (CWSS) of the Central and West Asia Department of the Asian Development Bank (ADB).

Contributions were received from team members: Eduardo Banzon (principal health specialist; Sustainable Development and Climate Change Department, ADB); and Grigor Gyurjan (senior economics officer, Armenia Resident Mission, ADB).

Gladys Ann Maravilla, Madeline Dizon, Cristina Lim, and Helen Grace Pingol provided support in preparing the report. Funding for this report is obtained from Armenia Transaction Technical Assistance and Regional Technical Assistance on Innovation headed by Susann Roth.

The team appreciates insightful comments from Triin Habicht, senior health economist, World Health Organization Barcelona Office for Health Systems Strengthening; Matthias Helble, economist, Economic Analysis and Operational Support Division, Economic Research and Regional Cooperation Department, ADB; and Nerses Yeritsyan, deputy governor, Central Bank of Armenia.

The team is indebted to the management for their support—Rie Hiraoka, director, CWSS; Shane Rosenthal, country director, Georgia Resident Mission; and Paolo Spantigati, country director, Armenia Resident Mission.

Abbreviations

ADB	–	Asian Development Bank
AMD	–	Armenian dram
BBP	–	Basic Benefit Package
COVID-19	–	coronavirus disease
CPI	–	consumer price index
FSU	–	former Soviet Union
GDP	–	gross domestic product
Global Fund	–	Global Fund to Fight AIDS, Tuberculosis and Malaria
IHME	–	Institute of Health Metrics and Evaluation
ILCS	–	Integrated Living Conditions Survey
IMF	–	International Monetary Fund
MOF	–	Ministry of Finance
MOH	–	Ministry of Health
MTEF	–	medium-term expenditure framework
OECD	–	Organisation for Economic Co-operation and Development
OOP	–	out-of-pocket
PHC	–	primary health care
PVHI	–	private voluntary health insurance
SHA	–	State Health Agency
SLAM	–	Simple Linear Actuarial Model
STHP	–	State Targeted Health Program
UHC	–	universal health coverage
UHI	–	universal health insurance
UN	–	United Nations
UNSTAT	–	United Nations Statistics Division
WEO	–	World Economic Outlook
WHO	–	World Health Organization

Executive Summary

Armenia is undertaking major health financing reforms to achieve universal health coverage (UHC) within the context of the Sustainable Development Goals and improving health system performance. These reforms are being implemented by completing the transformation from its historical Soviet-style health system to an incentivized and well-performing global best practice system, and by sustainably financing such efforts in light of their likely significant costs, other competing public priorities, and the country's future demographic transition and expected available fiscal space.

Armenia's actions for achieving these ends have been articulated in its recently enumerated Five-Year (2020–2025) Health Care System Development Strategy. In terms of health financing reform, the strategy proposes (i) implementing universal health care insurance through a unified single public fund, which will provide the entire population with a basic service package, funded through the state budget and a new health care tax; (ii) defining the basic service package in terms of reductions in the major burdens of disease and preventing impoverishment due to catastrophic illness costs; and (iii) purchasing services using modern performance-based methods that reflect real costs and technology changes.

This report attempts to develop an actuarial UHC costing model that relies on the most recent and complete health insurance claims data to estimate the likely incremental expenditures and revenue needs for achieving UHC. While there have been numerous studies of Armenia's health reform efforts, what has been lacking is a validated economic model to assess the likely increases in expenditures and revenue needs for the health financing reform policy options currently being developed to achieve UHC. The report describes the efforts of the Asian Development Bank to assist the government in the design, construction, calibration, evaluation, implementation, use, and refinement of such a model to assess the expenditure impacts and the implicit additional revenue requirements for financing alternative universal health insurance (UHI) policies.

The report focuses on the development and operationalization of this actuarial model as a tool for assessing the health financing and fiscal implications of Armenia's key UHI policy decisions. The focus of this report is on the construction of a flexible model based on Armenia's underly health system characteristics, demography, epidemiology, economy, and UHI policy choices. As greater future health and economic certainty evolve from the present coronavirus disease (COVID-19) crisis, model parameters, underlying data, and assumptions can be adjusted to reflect the latest Armenia-specific and global realities.

The government replaced Armenia's Soviet-era health system through a series of major legislative changes designed to provide publicly financed coverage for needed services focusing mainly on public health, emergency services, primary care, and specific social and catastrophic dread diseases. It also publicly funded insurance coverage for needy population groups (e.g., children, disabled, pensioners, the poor, etc.) and civil servants and military for most personal health services, while the remainder of the population has largely paid out-of-pocket (OOP) for personal health services not covered by the aforementioned universal basic public health and social/dread disease programs.

Armenia has an extensive, complicated, and interactive Basic Benefit Package (BBP) and administrative structure. It is complex to reform and creates major challenges for developing an actuarial costing model. This amalgam of eligibility, benefits, financing, provider payment, and delivery system interfaces is at the heart of both the system's strengths (focus on vulnerable groups and public health, relatively good health outcomes despite low public spending on health, progressive OOP payments) as well as its fundamental challenges. Challenges include chronic underfunding due to the extensive nature of the BBP and lack of health prioritization in the government budget; suboptimal health system performance due to lack of appropriate criteria for determining the BBP; high levels of OOP payments and total health spending resulting from low payment rates for socially vulnerable groups as well as half the population not being covered for comprehensive inpatient, drug, and certain diagnostic personal health services; lack of modern incentive-based payment systems; ineffective gatekeeper and referral arrangements, outdated treatment protocols and practice guidelines; lack of quality standards; and an inefficient delivery system configuration.

Armenia's overall health policy priorities are embodied in its draft 2020–2025 Health Sector Development Strategy and a recent draft UHI concept note posted by the government on 22 November 2019. Actual implementation and funding of government health programs are contained in its annual budgets and mapped into Armenia's medium-term expenditure framework (MTEF).

From an operational budget perspective, according to the MTEF 2020–2022, the main goals of the government health sector policies are the improved affordability and quality of health services, and improved health status of the population. The MTEF provides the projected 2020–2022 budget funding for the health sector. However, despite significant MTEF proposed increases in public spending on health, proposed allocations will result in an approximate budget share of only its current level (6%) in 2022. If one includes UHI implementation costs, the draft 2020–2025 Health Sector Development Strategy states that the necessary health budget share would need to be greater than 10% by 2025, while the aforementioned concept note estimates a requisite public budget share of about 11%. If implemented in 2021, both figures are well below the preliminary 13%–17% 2021 level projected by the actuarial model. Thus, implementation of UHI is likely to require significant additional future revenues from expected future fiscal space and/or new revenue sources entirely.

The current COVID-19 pandemic will likely have at least short- and perhaps medium-term impacts on health and other public spending needs and the country's ability to meet those needs arising from the pandemic, which will be reflected in future MTEFs. As of June 2020, the government is reallocating funding to hospitals treating COVID-19 patients, and has established a public extra-budgetary fund to help fund the unexpected treatment costs of the virus, while also dealing with the related health system impacts faced by other countries in terms of reduced demand for other non-COVID-19-related discretionary health service use.

According to the concept note policy, the new scheme aims to cover the formal sector and other privately employed individuals through a 6% earmarked payroll health tax, while the existing BBP beneficiaries including the Social Package (largely civil servants) and State Order (largely needy) groups will continue to be covered by public budget allocations, which, however, will be transformed from current direct service payments to providers to insurance premium payments to the proposed single-payer public agency (the UHI Fund). Thus, the health risks of both employer-insured and publicly covered beneficiaries will be pooled under the centralized and publicly managed health insurance fund. The proposal suggests implementation of a more unified benefits package for different categories of beneficiaries, improved remuneration rates and payment mechanisms for providers, and ability for the UHI Fund to exercise selective contracting of providers based on service quality assessments.

The design, costing, and the assessment of the proposed health financing reform policies and design and operationalization of the UHI actuarial costing model must be predicated on the country's current and future macro and fiscal health financing performance. This also includes underlying demographic, epidemiological, employment, and labor market trends and the availability of future fiscal space.

The main purpose of this report is to help the government in the design, construction, calibration, evaluation, implementation, use, and refinement of an Armenia-focused actuarial model to assess the expenditure impacts of alternative UHI policies. Given the concept note proposal to implement UHI through a government-financed single risk pool and/or purchaser public health insurance fund, the actuarial model focuses on estimating public expenditures. Comparing projected UHI expenditures with projected expenditures of the "current law" pre-UHI system provides an estimate of the incremental revenue needs to fund UHI.

The model for estimating future expenditures for both the pre-UHI system and possible future UHI alternatives is based on the latest available 2016 State Health Agency (SHA) claims data for Social Package and State Order groups. It is also based on Ministry of Health (MOH) and other government budget documents for estimating public spending on the universally available BBP benefits of primary care, public health/maternal and child health, emergency services, and socially important/dread disease programs, etc. The model uses the latest available demographic, labor market, and economic data for both baseline and future cost and enrollment projections.

However, the focus is the structural and functional specification of an Armenia-specific actuarial model to aid policymakers in UHI policy choices. The model is designed flexibly to accommodate better and more recent health insurance micro claims data as well as to accommodate updated past, current and future demographic, socioeconomic, epidemiological, labor market and (macro and micro) economic information from Armenian and international sources such as the United Nations, World Bank, International Monetary Fund (IMF), and WHO. Behavioral parameters such as demand- and supply-side responses to increased insurance coverage can be readily modified based on Armenia-specific and/or global experiences.

The cost estimation process involves two different sets of cost projections:

- The estimates show what future costs would have been had Armenia simply maintained its present pre-UHI system. One complication in specifying the pre-UHI baseline is how to handle the present post-2016 payment policy, which raised most of the State Order payment rates to Social Package levels. While this policy was not in place in 2016, it has been implemented subsequently in 2019. Since the costs of this policy are not trivial and UHI policies under consideration also appear to embody this change, pre-UHI baseline costs are estimated both exclusive (Scenario 1) and inclusive (Scenario 1a) of this change.

- The second set of projections uses the model to incorporate proposed changes in eligibility, benefits, and provider payment parameters embodied in suggested UHI proposals to estimate the costs of UHI in both the 2016 base year (Scenario 2) and its concept note proposed 2021 year of implementation (Scenario 4). By comparing the estimated pre-UHI baseline spending level in 2021 (e.g., Scenario 3) and the estimated UHI absolute spending levels in 2021 (e.g., Scenario 4), one obtains the incremental costs of implementing UHI relative to maintaining the pre-UHI baseline, thereby providing policymakers with estimates of both the absolute 2021 spending and needed revenue levels as well as the incremental expenditures and revenue needs to implement UHI.

The actuarial modeling of future public health expenditures is based on

- health utilization levels and trends;
- the benefit packages (i.e., health services that are covered, including whether there are copayments required);
- the demographics of the currently insured population and assumptions regarding enrollment of new groups and their demographic and socioeconomic situations;
- assumptions regarding population growth; and
- the cost of health services and overall cost trends.

Combining these leads to the actuarial estimates of health expenditures. Changes in expenditures from the pre-UHI baseline inform policymakers of future incremental and total expenditures and revenue needs.

The policy options directly amenable for analysis and explored in this report include

- changes in the benefit packages,
- changes in the definition of eligibility groups and enrollment of eligibility groups and subgroups,
- harmonization of health services cost reimbursements, and
- assessment of funding gaps.

The model scenarios in this report focus on the current baseline BBP and eligibility categories and the assessment of funding gaps. The model presented here is a first step in assisting the government in developing a permanent internal health financing modeling capacity. The substantial individual country and global health and economic consequences of the COVID-19 pandemic highlight the need to periodically update future demographic, socioeconomic, labor market, and economic trend information underlying the model as the current very high level of future economic uncertainty diminishes. There are two 2021 scenarios, which relate to 2016 pre-UHI/current system costs projected to 2021 and full 2021 UHI implementation costs.

The model is a flexible tool that can evaluate numerous health financing policy options implemented over various time periods. In this report, five illustrative scenarios are discussed. For model development and validation and policy relevance purposes, three 2016 baseline scenarios are analyzed, two relate to the pre-UHI 2016 baseline, and one assesses the costs in 2016 if UHI had been fully implemented that year. There are two 2021 scenarios, which relate to 2016 pre-UHI/current system costs projected to 2021 and full 2021 UHI implementation costs.

The pre-UHI scenarios are

- Scenario 1 for the actual 2016 pre-UHI baseline of no UHI and different payment rates for State Order and Social Package beneficiaries; and Scenario 1a, which is the same as Scenario 1, but evaluates what 2016 costs would have been if State Order payment rates were raised to Social Package payment levels. Scenario 1 is used to validate and calibrate the model by adjusting the parameters to assure estimates equate to the actual claims information as well as all government spending on health as reported in annual budget documents. Scenario 1a provides a useful order of magnitude estimate of the policy to raise State Order payment rates to the Social Package levels, this policy being a precursor to UHI, albeit not in place in 2016.

- Scenario 2 for 2016 shows what the costs of the concept note UHI proposal would have been if it had been fully implemented in 2016. This provides a useful validation for the proposed concept note 2021 implementation date estimate as it abstracts from projection errors from the 2016 base as well as possible changes in spending estimates due to demographic, socioeconomic, and macroeconomic factors including uncertainties in the 2020 and 2021 macroeconomic projections resulting from the COVID-19 pandemic. It is a simple, but useful validation of the likely magnitude of future projections, and provides a good *ceteris paribus* comparison for the 2016 pre-UHI baseline.

- Scenario 3 is simply the pre-UHI baseline Scenario 1a projected out to 2021. We use the pre-UHI baseline projections inclusive of the harmonized payment rates as those additional costs are already budgeted in the MTEF and are therefore part of the 2021 pre-UHI baseline spending. Thus, they should not be considered as an incremental cost of UHI in 2021.

- Scenario 4 assumes full UHI implementation in 2021 as proposed in the concept note.

Taken together, these scenarios provide estimates of the total costs and revenue needs for 2021, and the easily derived incremental costs of implementing UHI in 2021 versus staying with the pre-UHI baseline. Given the uncertainties and significant changes in the 2020 and (to a lesser extent) 2021 macroeconomic growth estimates resulting from the COVID-19 pandemic, we provide UHI estimates based on the pre-pandemic growth estimates, and perform a sensitivity analysis using the April 2020 pandemic inclusive IMF World Economic Outlook growth projections.

Given the lack of UHI BBP specificity in the existing government policy documents, it is assumed that for nonvulnerable and nonspecial needs groups (e.g., private formal sector workers) the UHI BBP is the Social Package BBP. For groups that fit into the 2016 special needs and vulnerable categories and are eligible for additional services, it is assumed that those groups will still be covered for their additional group benefits that were covered in 2016. In other words, everyone is either covered *de minimis* by the Social Package BBP and/or their more extensive 2016 vulnerability subgroup BBP.

While the present model does not have a dedicated revenue module, it provides information about the additional resources that will be needed to fully fund UHI. It also shows how additional expenditures and funding needs break out by eligibility groups and service categories. Therefore, it provides useful guidance to policymakers about possible revenue enhancement policies in terms of new or existing general (e.g., income, payroll, property, value added, excise) and earmarked taxes, voluntary or mandatory individual premiums (e.g., like the United States Medicare Part B program, where beneficiaries can pay a subsidized voluntary premium for outpatient services not covered elsewhere in the program), and/or cost-sharing.

A critically important policy outcome of expanding eligibility and benefits under UHI is that such expansions will reduce private OOP costs significantly (currently about 8% of [GDP]), over 80% of all health spending, and about 8% of all household spending). This considerably increases the ability to pay taxes and/or premiums for many non-vulnerable individuals and/or households, who would be among the major beneficiaries of the public UHI expansion.

In 2016, before implementation of UHI Scenario 1, total public health spending was about AMD88 billion, 6.1% of the public budget, and 1.75% of GDP. If in that same year State Order payment rates were raised to Social Package levels, Scenario 1a, public spending on health would have increased from AMD88 billion to AMD108 billion, a 23% increase; the public health share of the budget would have increased by 1.4 percentage points to 7.5%; and, the public health spending share of GDP would have increased by 0.4 percentage points to 2.1%. These are significant increases for this ongoing policy change, reflecting how out of line the base State Order payment rates were and may potentially still be.

If UHC had been fully implemented in 2016 from the actual 2016 Scenario 1 pre-UHI baseline without any increment to the public budget from additional health taxes, Scenario 2, public spending on health would have almost tripled from AMD88 billion to AMD251 billion (185% increase). The health budget share would have increased from 6.1% to 17.3% and the ratio of public spending on health to GDP would have increased from 1.75% to almost 5%. Even if the additional costs of the payment equalization, Scenario 1a, are factored in, spending would have increased by around AMD143 billion, a 132% increase.

These are enormous increases over and above actual 2016 public spending, which would undoubtedly be almost impossible to absorb without significant revenue enhancements or budget reprioritization. Much of the reason for this is the extensiveness of the current and proposed UHI BBP, low prioritization of health in the budget, the current low levels of comprehensive coverage for personal health services for non-vulnerable populations, low reimbursement rates, and the extremely high OOP costs faced by most Armenians, who are in effect funding these deficiencies in public spending on health through private household expenditures.

The 2021 concept note implementation Scenario 4 shows a similar picture. Assuming that the pre-UHI Scenario 3 in 2021 includes the equalization of payment rates, it is estimated that spending under the pre-UHI baseline in 2021 would be about AMD115 billion, while the implementation of UHI in 2021 (Scenario 4) would increase public spending on health to AMD279 billion, an increase of almost 150%, or 2.5 times the 2021 pre-UHI level in absolute terms, similar to the magnitudes found for the 2016 scenarios. The health budget share of the government budget would increase from 5.7% to 13.8%, and the GDP share for public spending on health from 1.5% to 3.7%.

One can also analyze spending increases by eligibility and benefit groups. Funding for most groups more than doubles under UHI in 2016 and 2021; however, for the pensioners and the everyone else groups, spending increases four- to fivefold, reflecting that 50% of the population currently without comprehensive coverage for personal health services and the large amounts of requisite OOP cost even for disadvantaged groups due to low payment rates. In terms of the different categories of benefits, as would be expected Social Package, State Order, and outpatient drugs show extremely large increases reflecting comprehensive coverage for largely uncovered people and for poorly covered benefits like outpatient drugs, which in fact account for the predominate share of overall OOP payments.

Armenia should have some moderate amounts of new fiscal space from projected 4%–5% growth over the medium term. But even assuming much of that went to health, it would not be enough to support public health spending increases of this magnitude. Besides, the government has several other competing priorities, and current spending plans undoubtedly will have to be adjusted to deal with the current COVID-19 pandemic and national and global economic crises.

The actuarial model should be refined and turned over to appropriate Armenian counterparts. If more recent claims data are available, the model should be rebased with these newer data. Refinements to the expenditure projections could better identify who benefits, their profiles, and their ability to pay. Knowing this will help in the design of a revenue module. Related to this is the need to have much more information about the details of the proposed UHI policies, because the current concept note is often vague about important policy parameters like standardization of the proposed BBP, cost-sharing, balanced billing, and the role of private voluntary insurance.

The model does not have a separate revenue module. The expenditure projections show the large incremental costs to implement UHI. It is also clear that many of the groups benefiting would be better-off formal private and informal sector workers, who currently are spending about 9% of their household budgets on health privately. The question is: What are the best options to raise additional revenues for health to fund UHI that are equitable, administrable, and nondistortionary to the economy, assure financial protection, raise sufficient revenues, and are sustainable? Further, are there combinations of changes in existing taxes, possibly new earmarked or unearmarked taxes (sugary beverages, carbon, financial transactions), and/or voluntary and/or mandatory individual insurance premiums that could be employed that are consistent with the government's tax policy reform directions?

OOP payment is currently above 80% of health spending and 8% of GDP. The UHI expansions will substantially reduce OOP payment for the population (e.g., especially for drugs, which account for some 39% of OOP cost), although the exact magnitude is difficult to estimate, and likely will disproportionately benefit non-vulnerable populations. Policies considered will need to support the government's future tax system vision as embodied in the MTEF and the IMF Article IV and Standby Program. Other sources of potential financing modalities that are not well articulated in the concept note or policy debate are efficiency gains, specific results-based provider payment, referral system and gatekeeper policies, practice guidelines and treatment protocols, delivery system rationalization to eliminate the inpatient bias, and rationalization of the very comprehensive BBP based on efficiency, affordability, sustainability and catastrophic protection criteria.

It is recommended that the government formally establish a high-level task force composed of members from the Ministry of Finance, Ministry of Economy, MOH, Central Bank, the Ministry of Labor and Social Affairs, and other relevant stakeholders. The task force could focus holistically on Armenia's overall health reform efforts including health financing, delivery system rationalization, pharmaceuticals, health information systems, etc. Indeed the ongoing COVID-19 debate has highlighted the need to holistically consider health system reforms in terms of all aspects of health systems along with interactive non-health sector related programs, significantly complicating budget prioritization and fiscal space considerations. Alternatively, if the government feels a more targeted focus on health financing is more appropriate, the task force could focus on the key unresolved health financing issues, some of which are not addressed in detail in the concept note. This could also include alternative revenue sources, simplification of the eligibility criteria, rationalization of the BBP, specific performance-based payment systems, and the role and regulation of private health insurance. A public process such as this could both educate the public and help garner support for the reform, particularly in complex areas such as the potentially large reductions in OOP payments being used to help finance UHI.

Armenia's health system is unique in both its high level of overall health spending and its extremely heavy reliance on OOP payments, which both deprives the government of needed revenues and its citizens of the financial protection and equity embodied in sharing risks through a public insurance mechanism. Furthermore, it also limits the government's financial leverage over the system. While Armenia's system is designed to help the poor and vulnerable, it needs to transform itself into an efficient and appropriately funded UHI scheme providing access and financial protection for the entire population.

One major financial challenge in this transition is to assure adequate public funding of UHI by transforming much of the 8% of GDP going to OOP payments and 8% of household budgets being spent on health into additional public resources to support UHI. Having detailed actuarial estimates of the costs of UHI and who will benefit from its implementation provides important information for effectuating this complex funding transition.

CHAPTER I

Introduction

Armenia is undertaking major health financing reforms to achieve universal health coverage (UHC) within the context of the Sustainable Development Goals. Armenia is improving performance in its health sector by completing its transformation from its historical Soviet-style health system to an incentivized and well-performing global best practice system. The country will be financing these efforts in light of their likely significant costs, other competing public priorities, and the country's expected available future fiscal space and its medium-term expenditure framework (MTEF). Developing effective reform policies requires understanding of both key UHC health policy reform elements, as well as political economic assessments of the performance of Armenia's baseline health system. The reform policies will be further assessed in terms of how well they achieve the basic health system goals of maximizing health outcomes, assuring financial protection against poverty, providing equity and efficiency in use and financing, and consumer responsiveness in the context of Armenia's current and future demographics, epidemiological trends, and likely available future fiscal space. All of these efforts are further complicated by the major health and economic uncertainties resulting from the coronavirus disease (COVID-19) pandemic.

While there have been numerous studies of Armenia's health reform efforts,[1] what has been lacking is a validated economic model that assesses the likely increases in expenditures and revenue needs for the health financing reform policy options. This report attempts to fill this void by helping develop an actuarial UHC costing model relying on the most recent and complete health insurance claims data to estimate the likely overall costs and costs by population subgroups and benefit categories for achieving UHC. This information can then be used to inform health financing reform options concerning both the scope and timing of eligibility expansions, Basic Benefit Package (BBP) composition and changes, changes in provider payment rates, and potential expenditure and revenue needs and sources to fund such proposed expansions in future MTEFs. This report does not focus on parallel delivery system and governance changes but will account for key interactive health system elements affecting UHC costs such as supply response, unmet needs, and pharmaceutical pricing and industry policies.

---

[1] See E. Richardson. 2013. Armenia: Health System Review. *Health Systems in Transition.* 15(4):1–99.; R. Lavado, S. Hayrapetyan, and S. Kharazyan. 2018. Expansion of the Benefit Package: The Experience of Armenia. *Universal Health Care Coverage Series* No. 27. Washington, DC: World Bank Group.

The report focuses on the development and implementation of an actuarial model as a tool for assessing the health financing and fiscal implications of Armenia's key universal health insurance (UHI) policy decisions. The empirical health policy results depend on underlying past, present, and future demographic, socioeconomic, labor market, health financing, and macroeconomic trends as well as specific model parameter choices (e.g., demand and supply responses to increased insurance coverage), and future projections of which at this time are in great flux and uncertainty as a result of the COVID-19 pandemic. The focus of this report is on the construction of a flexible model based on Armenia's underlying health system, demography, epidemiology, economy, and UHI policy levers. As greater future health and economic certainty evolve from the present national and global pandemic and economic crises, model parameters and assumptions can be adjusted to reflect the latest Armenian and global economic and health realities.

Key to the development of effective UHC policy options and model specification is an understanding of the structural features and overall performance of the current health financing system. Assessing such performance in the context of the system's historical institutional evolution informs actuarial model and financing options design.

This introductory chapter sets the stage for these efforts by providing an overview and summary performance assessment of the Armenian health financing system in terms of its overall health financing features and goals of improving health outcomes, assuring financial protection against poverty, assuring equity in contributions and benefits, promoting access and quality, assuring efficiency in financing and service delivery, and assuring the future financial sustainability of the system. Chapter II discusses in detail the historical evolution of Armenia's health system. Chapter III further elaborates on this evolution by providing a detailed description of the key government-funded health programs, the underlying parameters of which serve as the building blocks for the actuarial model. Chapter IV highlights the key UHC health financing policy reform options currently under consideration by the government based on the system's complex eligibility, benefit, revenue, and provider payment structures. Chapter V describes the basic model, its underlying data, basic parameter estimates, validation procedures, and limitations. In Chapter VI, the model provides estimates for several different health reform policy scenarios. These results are analyzed in detail and discussed in the context of future demographic and epidemiological trends, other competing public priorities, and likely available future fiscal space. Chapter VII discusses possible refinements to the model for better accuracy, expansion to other health policy areas, and potential foci for Armenia's future health policy reform processes.

Comparative Performance Assessment of Armenia's Health Financing System Although various studies have assessed the Armenian health system, few have relied on the latest national health expenditure, demographic, and updated macroeconomic and micro survey data. Few have tried to relate micro survey data and macro trends in key health financing parameters to Armenia's health financing performance relative to other comparable income countries in terms of public and private health spending levels and rates of change, budget prioritization of health, and financial protection and equity.[2] For its spending and income levels, Armenia's health outcomes are generally better than

---

[2]   Elsewhere we have also assessed performance against inputs and health outcomes, where Armenia does reasonably well vis-à-vis health outcomes relative to public and private spending levels but tends to have more physical inputs than other comparable income countries.

average, but it uses higher levels of inputs than its income comparators.[3] From the perspective of consumer responsiveness and forgoing needed care, only half of the population is satisfied with their latest hospital visit, and around 40% are satisfied with their primary health care (PHC). Around 24% of the lowest quintile reported not seeking care due to affordability issues.[4]

1. Summary of Macro Health Financing Trends

- Armenia's total health spending is high by international standards with the health sector accounting for about 10% of the economy, 3–4 percentage points higher than in comparable income countries and similar to European Union levels (Figure 1).[5]
- Yet, OOP payments for health are over 80% of all health spending and well above the World Health Organization's (WHO) proposed 20% threshold, increasing, and the highest in the world (Figure 2) (footnote 5).

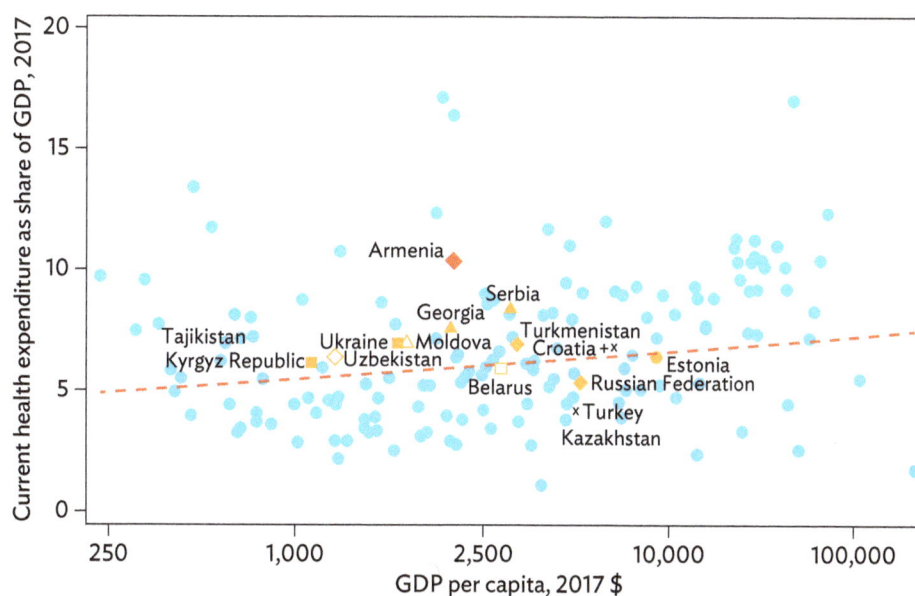

Figure 1: Current Health Expenditure as Share of GDP, 2017

GDP = gross domestic product.
Source: World Development Indicators database.

[3] M. Jowett. 2016. *Why Does UHC Performance Vary So Much Across Countries, At Any Given Level of Health Spending?* PowerPoint presentation prepared for GIZ Symposium, Retreat on Health, Social Protection and Inclusion. Germany. 8 September. http://health.bmz.de/events/Events_2015/A_Retreat_on_Health__Social_Protection_and_Inclusion_2016/06_breakout_1_5/Jowett_break_out_session_8_Sept_2016.pdf.
[4] Figures derived from Statistical Committee of the Republic of Armenia. 2018. *Integrated Living Conditions Survey 2017 micro dataset.* https://www.armstat.am/en/?nid=205 (accessed 3 January 2020).
[5] World Health Organization. 2020. *Global Health Expenditure Database.* https://apps.who.int/nha/database/Select/Indicators/en (accessed 3 January 2020).

Figure 2: Out-of-Pocket Payments as Share of Current Health Expenditure (2017)

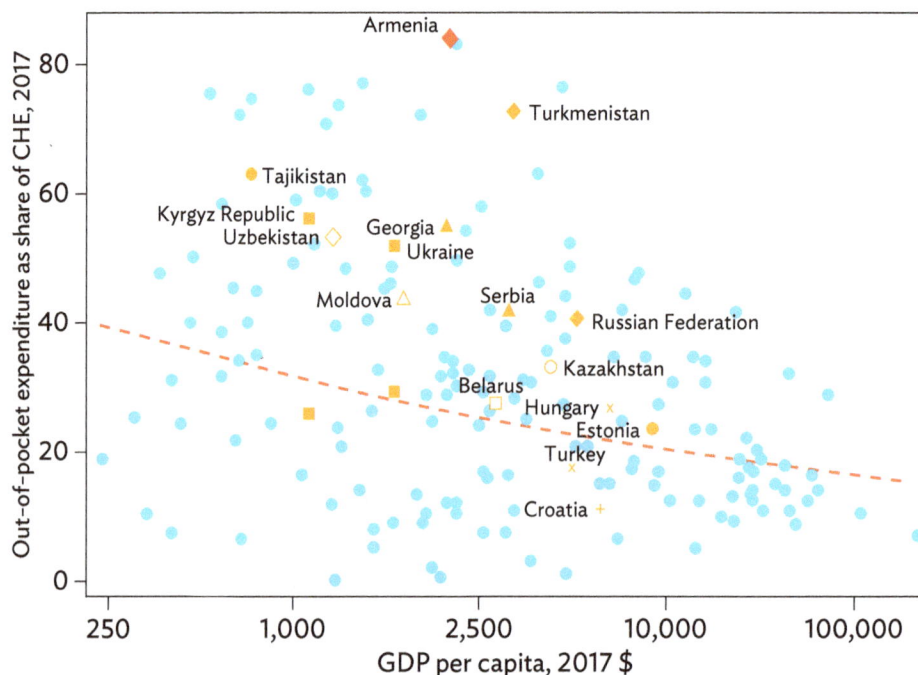

GDP = gross domestic product.
Source: World Development Indicators database.

- While OOP payment is progressive with, higher income groups spending a larger proportion of their household spending on health, it is not clear if the poor are simply benefiting from effective public system targeting and/or simply cannot afford to seek privately financed care (Figure 3). Around 24% of the lowest quintile did not seek medical care when sick due to affordability issues. About 39% of these OOP payments are for medicines, but about 35% are also for hospital services, even for low-income groups who are supposedly publicly insured for these services.[6]
- Armenia does not prioritize health in its budget, dedicating some 6% of its public budget to health, 2–3 percentage points less than global comparators, thus precluding effective financial protection, risk sharing, and redistribution (Figure 4).
- Public risk sharing on health is less than 2% of GDP, well below the 5% recommended WHO threshold, limiting effective risk sharing, financial protection, and redistribution (Figure 5).[7]

---

[6] National Institute of Health. 2020. *2019 National Health Accounts.* Yerevan. http://nih.am/assets/pdf/atvk/3a71b247c965d4cce6002a3229447583.pdf

[7] World Health Organization. 2020. Global Health Expenditure Database. https://apps.who.int/nha/database/Select/Indicators/en (accessed 3 January 2020); International Monetary Fund. 2020. *World Economic Outlook Databases.* https://www.imf.org/en/Publications/SPROLLs/world-economic-outlook-databases#sort=%40imfdate%20descending (accessed 3 January 2020), and World Bank. 2020. World Development Indicators. https://datacatalog.worldbank.org/dataset/world-development-indicators (accessed 3 January 2020).

Figure 3: Out-of-Pocket Payments as Percentage of Total Household Expenditure (2017)

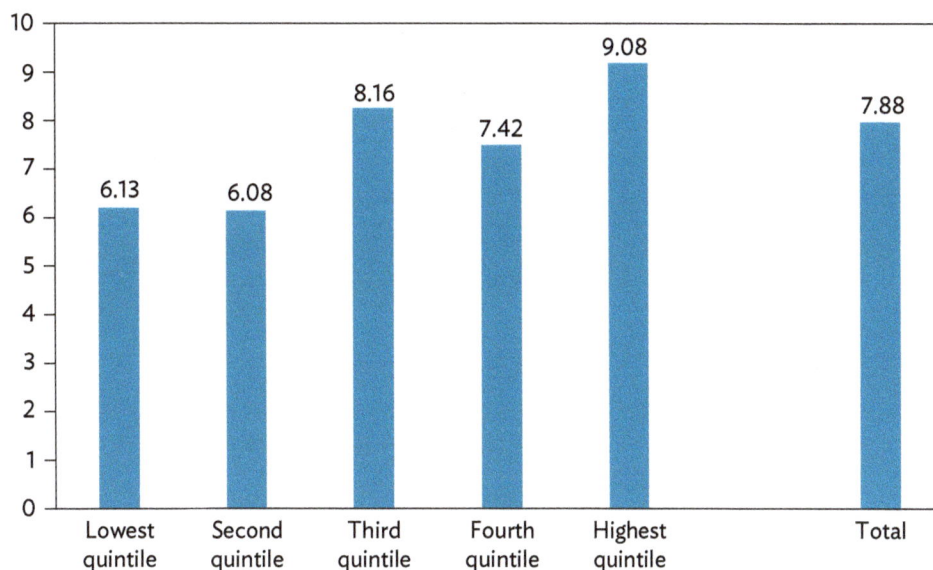

Source: Integrated Living Conditions Survey, 2017.

Figure 4: Domestic Public Health Expenditure as Share of the Budget, 2017

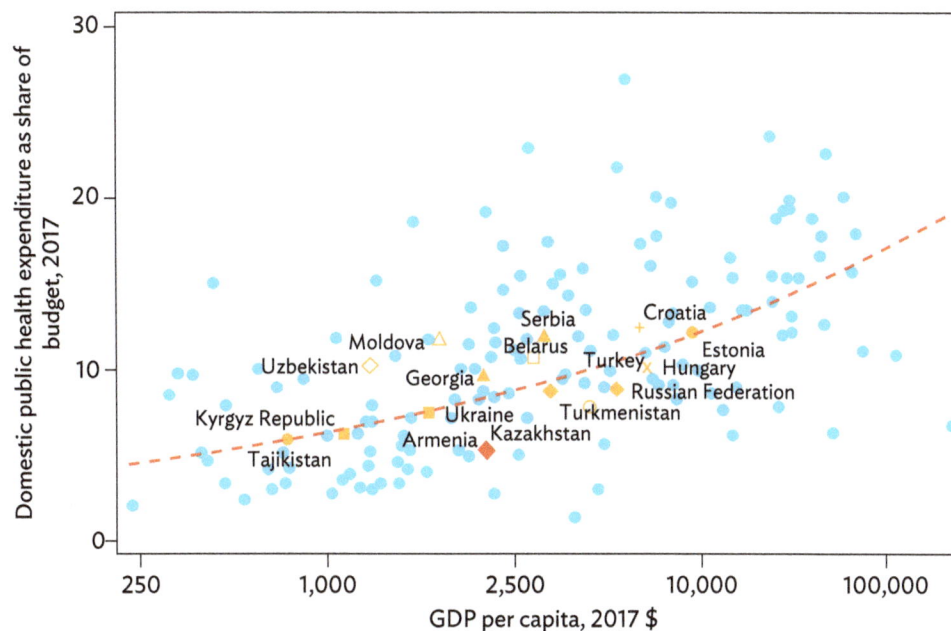

GDP = gross domestic product.
Source: World Development Indicators database.

Figure 5: Domestic Public Health Expenditure as Share of Gross Domestic Product, 2017

GDP = Gross domestic product.
Source: World Development Indicators database.

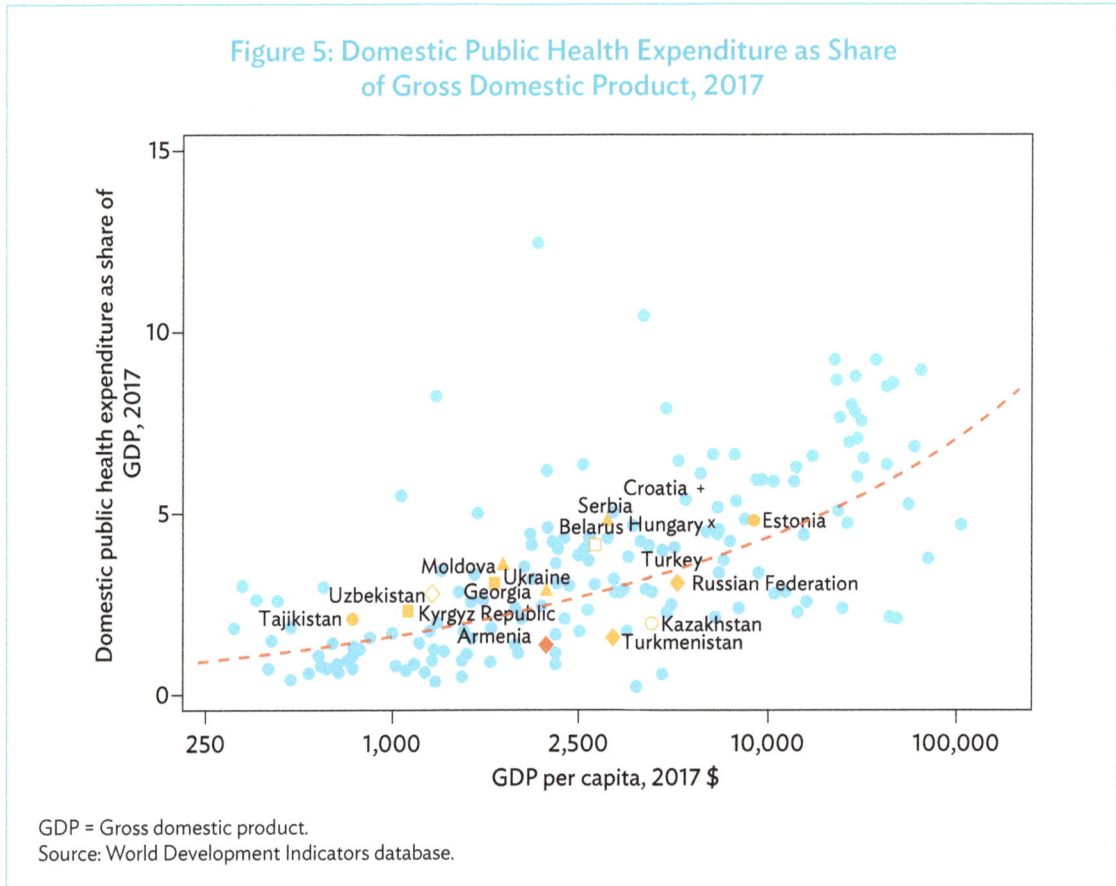

- Public spending on health has not kept pace with growth in overall government spending or GDP, resulting in OOP payments being an increasingly larger share of total health spending (Table 1).
- If one relates absolute increases in health spending to increases in GDP, increases in overall government spending, and increases in the share of overall government expenditures devoted to health (i.e., prioritization), low prioritization of health spending has contributed negatively to relative health spending growth for both the entire 2005– 2018 and the post-2008 financial crisis periods (Figure 6).
- The current eligibility criteria and benefit packages for public coverage focus on individuals, not families or households, and result in poor targeting of some needy groups, high administrative costs, and a complicated benefit structure, often incomprehensible to providers as well as beneficiaries.
- About 50% of the population lack comprehensive health coverage for hospital services under the BBP.[8]

---

[8]   R. Lavado, S. Hayrapetyan, and S. Kharazyan. 2018. Expansion of the Benefit Package: The Experience of Armenia. *Universal Health Care Coverage Series*. No. 27. Washington, DC: World Bank Group.

Table 1: Armenia's Pre-Reform Health Expenditure Baseline, 2005–2018

Year	Current Health Spending (% of GDP)	OOP (% of GDP)	Domestic Public Spending on Health (% of CHE)	Domestic Private Spending on Health as % of CHE	External Spending on Health (% of CHE)	OOP on Health (% of CHE)	CHE Per Capita (PPP)	CHE Per Capita ($)	CHE Per Capita (AMD)	Domestic Public Spending on Health (% of GGE)
2005	5.8	3.7	30.9	64.3	4.9	64.3	273	94	45,017	8.9
2010	9.1	7.2	19.9	78.6	1.6	78.6	600	294	140,800	6.9
2014	10.2	8.4	14.8	83.7	1.5	78.8	828	392	187,735	6.2
2015	10.1	8.3	16.7	82.5	0.8	81.6	858	355	170,047	6.1
2016	9.9	8.0	17.4	81.3	1.3	80.6	860	351	168,098	6.1
2017	10.4	8.8	14.1	85.1	0.8	84.3	982	401	192,043	5.4
2018	10.0	8.8	13.1	86.2	0.7	80.8	1,024	420	202,855	5.5

AMD = Armenian dram ($1 = AMD478.905 as of 3 January 2020), CHE = current health expenditure, GDP = gross domestic product, GGE = general government expenditure, OOP = out-of-pocket payments, PPP = United States dollar purchasing power parity.

Notes: (i) Current total health spending at 10% of GDP is 4.2% of GDP higher in 2018 than it was in 2005; (ii) The single largest source of health spending at 81% is unpooled OOP payments, well above the WHO 20% threshold recommended for effective financial protection; (iii) Public spending on health accounts for only 13% of current health spending, some 1.5% of GDP;

(iv) The share of the government budget allocated to health is only 5.5%, (i.e., 3.4% less than it was in 2005, raising questions of societal prioritization of health.

Sources: Armenia National Health Accounts (NHA) 2018; World Development Indicators database. https://databank.worldbank.org/reports.aspx?source=World-Development-Indicators; Armenia Government Financial Statistics Website 2019.

Figure 6: Prioritization for Health, 2018

Armenia (2008)

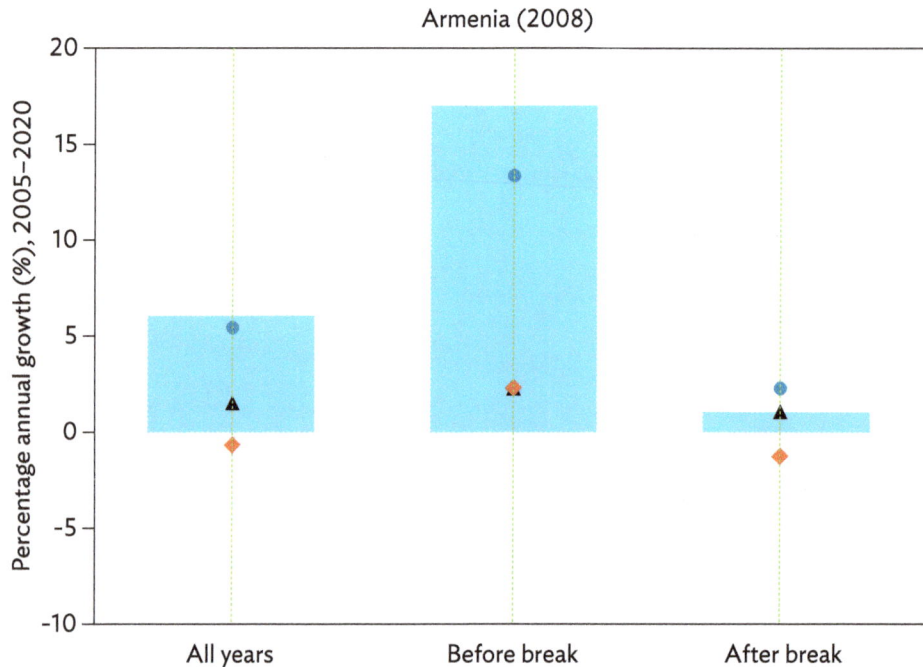

Notes: Blue circle denotes economic growth expressed as changes in GDP per capita; black triangle denotes aggregate public spending expressed as changes in aggregated public expenditures as share of GDP; and orange diamond denotes reprioritization expressed as changes in health's share in aggregate public expenditure.

Source: A. Tandon et al. 2018. Intertemporal Dynamics of Public Financing for Universal Health Coverage: Accounting for Fiscal Space Across Countries. *Health, Nutrition and Population Discussion Papers*. Washington, DC: World Bank. https://openknowledge.worldbank. org/handle/10986/31211.

2.   Armenia's Challenging Demographic, Epidemiological, Labor Market, Industrial Structure, and Socioeconomic Constraints

- Armenia's youth dependency ratio will continue to decline, while the aged and overall dependency ratios are increasing, resulting in fewer workers to support each dependent person (48 dependents per 100 workers in 2020 vs 61 dependents per 100 workers in 2050, a 27% increase in dependency of largely high-cost elderly individuals).[9]
- The employment rate is low (50%)[10,] and the unemployment rate remains among the highest in the Europe and Central Asia region (18%), largely stemming from low job creation and a mismatch of workers' skills and jobs.[11]

---

[9]   UNSTAT. Demographic Statistics Database. http://data.un.org/Data.aspx?d=POP&f=tableCode%3A2 (accessed 2 January 2020).

[10]   Statistical Committee of the Republic of Armenia. 2018. Integrated Living Conditions Survey 2017 microdata set. https://www. armstat.am/en/?nid=205 (accessed 3 January 2020).

[11]   Statistical Committee of the Republic of Armenia. 2018. Social Snapshot and Poverty in Armenia, 2008–2017 https://www. armstat.am/file/article/poverty_2018_english_2.pdf (accessed 3 January 2020).

Table 2: Dependency Ratios, 2010–2050

Year	Youth	Old	Total
2010	28	16	44
2020	30	18	48
2030	25	26	51
2040	22	29	51
2050	24	37	61

Source: UNSTAT, latest year. https://population.un.org/wpp/Download/Standard/Population/.

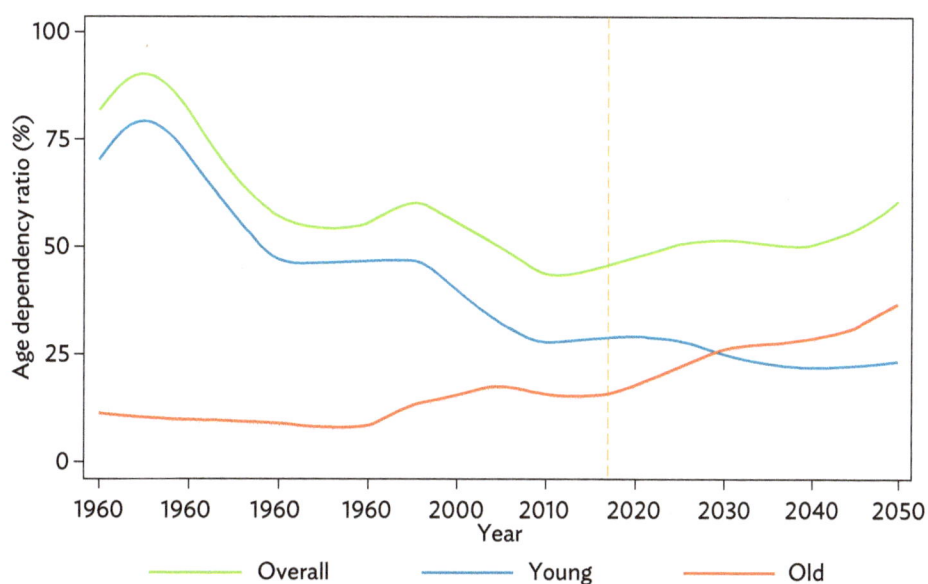

Figure 7: Dependency Ratio Trends, 1960–2050

Source: UNSTAT, latest data https://population.un.org/wpp/Download/Standard/Population/.

- About 25% percent of workers are in low wage occupations, and 17% of households do not have an employed household member (footnote 10).
- Informality is high, accounting for some half (47%) of all employment and over 18% of non-agricultural employment (footnote 10).
- About 25% of the population is poor (footnote 11), and current targeting is problematic due to inclusion and exclusion errors.

3.   Armenia's Future Available Fiscal Space and Sustainability Is Somewhat Limited

- Fiscal space[12] is defined as "…room in a government's budget that allows it to provide resources for a desired purpose without jeopardizing the sustainability of its financial position or the stability of the economy."[13]
- Sustainability is the capacity of a government, at least in the future, to finance its desired expenditure programs, to service any debt obligations (including those that may arise if the created fiscal space arises from government borrowing), and to ensure its solvency.
- There are five elements of fiscal space:

  (i)   increasing government revenues due to conducive economic conditions,
  (ii) increasing sovereign debt,
  (iii) higher levels of foreign aid,
  (iv) reprioritizing some sectors over others, and
  (v) increased efficiency of existing outlays.

- There should be some additional government revenues from Armenia's projected 4%–5% medium-term GDP growth, which may be enhanced by concomitant revenue administration and tax reforms. However, uncertainties regarding increased public program costs and short-term growth reductions due to the COVID-19 pandemic may reduce the magnitude of these currently projected future fiscal space potentials. Figures 8A and 8B show the IMF October 2019 World Economic Outlook (WEO) and Regional Economic Outlook (REO) GDP growth projections and the post-pandemic April and May IMF WEO and IMF Standby Program projections. Except for the negative 2020 GDP growth affecting virtually all countries, the 2021–2024 medium-term GDP projections for Armenia are basically the same.[14]
- A similar picture emerges for Armenia's continuing projected negative short- and medium-term fiscal balances (Figures 9A and 9B). While the 2020–2022 MTEF includes significant absolute increases in public health spending, the health budget share continues to decline, as these funds are earmarked to improve the current programs, not to support major proposed UHC coverage expansions. Moreover, budget reallocations to support pandemic treatments further reduce short-term fiscal space for other health or non-health-related budget activities.

[12]   This fiscal space analysis is based on the pre-pandemic October 2019 macro data from the REO and WEO. The 2020 April WEO and REO pandemic-based IMF projections as well as those in the IMF's May 2020 Republic of Armenia Second Review Under the Stand-By Arrangement document suggest negative growth in 2020 of 1%–2% with a return to the previously projected 2021–2024 4% –5% growth levels. Since except for the negative 2020 growth figure, the outyears are more or less similar for Armenia and most of the countries, and there is a large uncertainty in these latest projections as we are only in the initial or mid-phase of the pandemic, we present here the fiscal space analysis based on the pre-pandemic projections, which were also the bases for the MTEF and Armenian health policy decisions. Also as shown in Table 15, Chapter 6, use of the pandemic-based April 2020 IMF macro projections has virtually no impact on the 2021 UHI cost projections relative to the pre-pandemic macro data.

[13]   P. Heller. 2005. Fiscal Space: What it is and how to get it. *Finance and Development.* 42 (2).

[14]   IMF. 2020. World Economic Outlook Databases. https://www.imf.org/en/Publications/SPROLLs/world-economic-outlook-databases#sort=%40imfdate%20descending (accessed 3 January 2020).

Figure 8: Armenia's Projected Growth in Gross Domestic Product, 2005–2024

IMF Pre-Pandemic, October 2019
(WEO or REO)

IMF Pandemic-Influenced, April/May 2020
(WEO Standby Program)

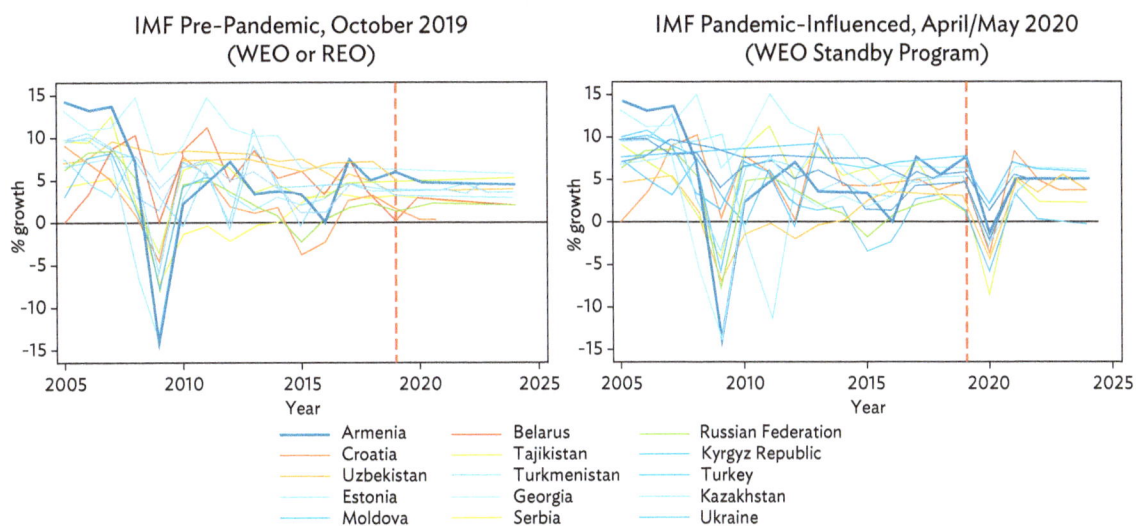

Armenia	Belarus	Russian Federation
Croatia	Tajikistan	Kyrgyz Republic
Uzbekistan	Turkmenistan	Turkey
Estonia	Georgia	Kazakhstan
Moldova	Serbia	Ukraine

IMF = International Monetary Fund, REO = Regional Economic Outlook, WEO = World Economic Outlook.
Source: IMF.

Figure 9: Armenia's Projected Fiscal Balance, 2005–2024

IMF Pre-Pandemic, October 2019
(WEO or REO)

IMF Pandemic-Influenced, April/May 2020
(WEO Standby Program)

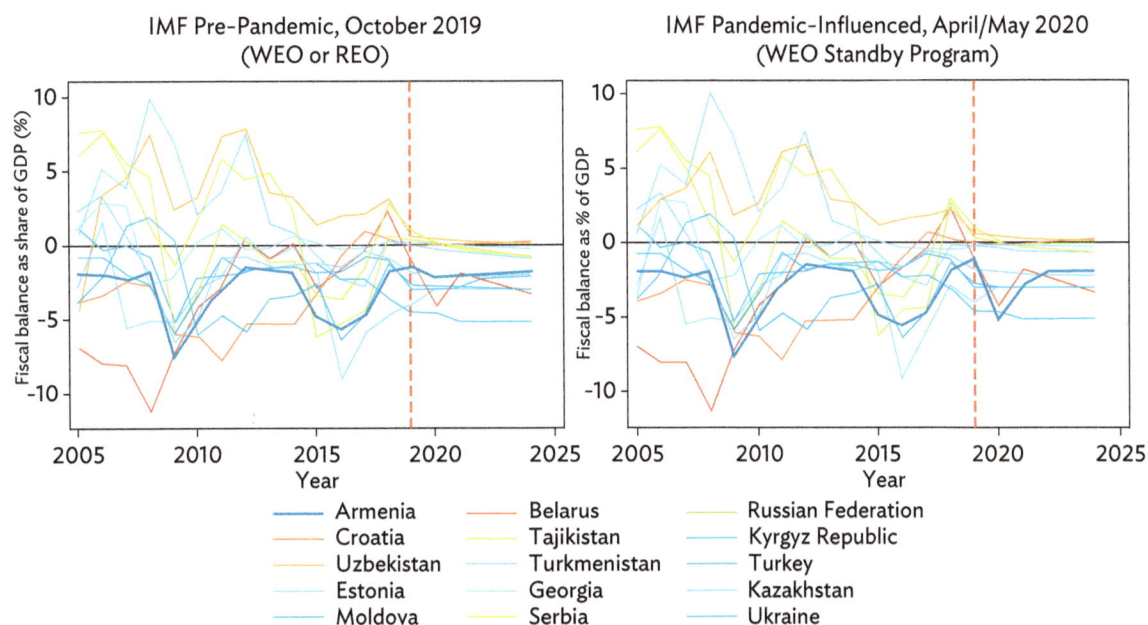

Armenia	Belarus	Russian Federation
Croatia	Tajikistan	Kyrgyz Republic
Uzbekistan	Turkmenistan	Turkey
Estonia	Georgia	Kazakhstan
Moldova	Serbia	Ukraine

IMF = International Monetary Fund, REO = Regional Economic Outlook, WEO = World Economic Outlook.
Source: IMF.

- Thus, the overall fiscal space situation is both somewhat uncertain but mixed:

  (i) Increasing sovereign debt through borrowing is highly unlikely given the MTEF, new fiscal rules, and the IMF program, as there are significant penalties to increasing the debt above its current 50% level.[15]

  (ii) Obtaining higher levels of foreign assistance is also unlikely as the Global Fund to Fight AIDS, Tuberculosis and Malaria (Global Fund) and other donors' transition away from Armenia as its income moves up in the middle-income country range.

  (iii) Given the relatively low level of prioritization of health in the budget at about 6%,[16] if MOH can demonstrate high rates of return on future public health spending and some way to capture or diminish the 8% of GDP currently going into the health sector from private OOP payments, it should be able to make the case for significantly greater prioritization of health in the budget.

  (iv) Earmarked taxes (e.g., tobacco and alcohol), taxes on formal sector workers and employers, tax subsidies to purchase social health insurance, and mandated individual premiums are all potential mechanisms for increasing public revenues for health. However, the Ministry of Finance (MOF) and Central Bank of Armenia (CBA) will need to weigh each of these in the context of ongoing tax reform and overall fiscal management perspectives, including the negative fiscal balance and high level of informality.

  (v) Efficiency gains in health or other social sectors are one of the most likely sources of future fiscal space, especially given the numerous inefficiencies in the current Armenia financing and delivery systems, including lack of performance-based payment systems, inpatient care biases, excess bed and workforce capacity, lack of payment rules on the private sector, etc.

4.   The Reform Baseline: Strengths and Weaknesses of the Current System

- The strengths of the current system include the following:

  (i) Public spending is low relative to global comparators, while health outcomes are relatively good.

  (ii) The entire population is covered for primary care, emergency services, and certain catastrophic or dread diseases free of charge, and the poor, other disadvantaged groups, and public employees are also covered for most curative care.

  (iii) Despite the high OOP payments, it accrues mostly to the nonpoor.[17]

  (iv) Having a single risk pool and purchaser through the State Health Agency (SHA) is conceptually a good global practice on both risk pooling and purchasing potential grounds.

  (v) The current situation of provider autonomy embodies the purchaser–provider split needed for implementation of modern performance-based, integrated care, payment systems.

---

[15]   IMF. 2020. World Economic Outlook Databases. https://www.imf.org/en/Publications/SPROLLs/world-economic-outlook databases#sort=%40imfdate%20descending (accessed 3 January 2020).

[16]   WHO. 2020. Global Health Expenditure Database. https://apps.who.int/nha/database/Select/Indicators/en (accessed 3 January 2020).

[17]   While the higher income quintiles are paying a higher share of their household incomes on health, this could reflect either relatively good income targeting regarding the BBP and/or simply the fact that the poor cannot afford to spend for critically needed health services privately. It is difficult to ascertain progressivity without looking at financial protection and unmet need together.

- The weaknesses of current system include the following:

    (i)   While the country devotes one-tenth of its economy to health, over 80% of that is through unpooled OOP private spending, denying the population equitable and effective insurance and financial protection.[18]

    (ii)   Armenia's OOP payment burden is the highest in the world, and four times the 20% WHO-recommended threshold for effective financial protection.

    (iii)   Medicines account for about 39% of the OOP payment burden for almost all income groups, because public coverage of medicines is limited to a small group of socially important diseases. Even for certain vulnerable population groups, where drugs that are listed on the Armenian Essential Medicines List are in principle distributed free of charge, most patients access medicines through the private sector, where prices are unregulated.

    (iv)   With about half of the population lacking effective publicly-funded coverage for personal curative care, the costs of UHC for the entire population may be prohibitive assuming appropriate provider payment levels, the extensiveness of the current BBP, low provider payment rates, and other inherent inefficiencies in the current purchasing arrangements and delivery system.

    (v)   Targeting is problematic and many poor people are not covered for the full BBP, while some nonpoor are erroneously classified as needy and covered.

    (vi)   As is the case in many former Soviet Union (FSU) countries, the service delivery system, despite important reforms, is still often inefficient, largely hospital-focused, and with no overall strategy to drive higher efficiency.

    (vii)   There is a lack of effective referral and gatekeeper systems.

    (viii) Private health insurance is very limited and poorly regulated.

    (ix)   Technology changes, rising incomes, and the demographic, epidemiological, and nutrition transitions will exert strong future cost pressures, resulting in fewer working age individuals to support an increasingly dependent and costly aging population.[19]

    (x)   Current reimbursement rates, both for the BBP and services paid OOP, are not based on the efficient costs of healthcare provision, nor have proper actuarial projections been made for future costs and/or to compare different cost-effective benefit packages for population subgroups or the whole population.

In addition to empirically understanding the overall health financing system performance, model design and financing reform options specification require an in-depth understanding of the institutional details of the health financing system and how it has evolved policy-wise and institutionally over time. The subsequent chapters attempt to provide this perspective.

---

[18]   WHO. 2020. Global Health Expenditure Database https://apps.who.int/nha/database/ Select/Indicators/en (accessed 3 January 2020); and National Institute of Health. 2020. 2019 *National Health Accounts*. Yerevan. http://nih.am/assets/pdf/atvk/3a71b247 c965d4cce6002a3229447583.pdf.

[19]   These are mostly outside the purview of the health system, but significantly affect the pursuit of UHC.

CHAPTER II

Historical Evolution of Armenia's Health Financing and Delivery Systems

Over the past 25 years, Armenia's health system has evolved from a standard Semashko Soviet national health service model that provided universal coverage through access to government-funded, owned, and operated facilities, and where medical staff were all public employees and paid through line item budgets—to a system that embodies choice, market incentives, and cost-sharing, with a publicly funded Basic Benefit Package (BBP) managed through a single purchaser—the State Health Agency (SHA).

The original legislation establishing SHA conceptually seemed to establish a single-purchaser agency to administer the new public financing system in the context of autonomous or privatized facilities, a purchaser–provider split, significant rationalization of an over-resourced delivery system, and the movement toward the use of modern efficiency-based purchasing arrangements including performance-based remuneration mechanisms. In practice, SHA was not empowered to perform the revenue-raising, risk-pooling, and purchasing functions of a modern health financing system. Its authorities have been progressively diminished over time. These health financing functions are largely performed by the Ministry of Health (MOH) rather than SHA, as SHA simply acts as an MOH department without independent decision-making rights.

Armenia's transition has been challenging. It has been affected by wars, natural disasters, refugee crises, the collapse of virtually all former Soviet Union (FSU) economies in the 1990s, the global financial crisis, cyclical changes in global commodity prices affecting Armenia's limited exports, internal politics, outmigration of skilled health professionals, and significant Armenian and global economic uncertainties from the global coronavirus disease (COVID-19) pandemic.

Armenia's Soviet-era health system suffered from the same problems as all FSU health systems—guaranteed free access to (theoretically) all needed services for the entire population funded with no cost-sharing from the public budget; severe underfunding of health, which was viewed as an unproductive sector; large numbers of low quality and poorly paid inputs organized on the basis of outmoded and ineffective planning norms; focus on inpatient over outpatient care; outdated public health and medical practice guidelines, including little attention to the impending noncommunicable disease burden; relatively poor health outcomes; high levels of under-the-table payments; and lack of incentives for efficiency, quality, and outcomes.

As its economy and health system collapsed following the breakup of the FSU, Armenia has implemented key legislative and policy reforms designed to provide publicly financed coverage to its population for needed services. These reforms focused mainly on public health, emergency services, and specific communicable and catastrophic dread diseases. It has also funded full coverage for needy population groups (e.g., children, disabled, pensioners, the poor) and civil servants and military for most personal health services. The remainder of the population has largely paid out-of-pocket (OOP) for personal health services not covered as basic public health, emergency, or catastrophic or dread disease-related services. The government has also rationalized the delivery system and eliminated some excess capacity, autonomized, and privatized much of the delivery system, and put in place elements of modern incentive-based provider payment systems.

In particular, the 1995 Constitution of Armenia guarantees universal entitlement to medical services funded by the state. However, economic realities resulted in several seminal events including adoption of the law on Medical Aid and Service of the Population in 1996, which laid the basis for some of the most important financing and delivery system reforms underpinning the current health system configuration. These included establishing universal access to a BBP of targeted public programs and personal health services as well as major changes in public ownership and control of health service delivery.

The Government of Armenia has also implemented other key healthcare reforms since the 1990s. This included reforming the primary health care (PHC) system through implementation of family medicine models and optimization of the hospital network. Between 1990 and 2017, the total number of hospital beds in Armenia has reduced by almost 60% and the number of hospitals by around 30%, while the number of PHC facilities has stayed relatively stable. The policy of health infrastructure optimization, implemented since the mid-2000s, has resulted in the closure of rural hospitals (most of which were transformed into rural PHC centers) and in merging most of the regional urban PHC facilities and maternity hospitals into regional health centers. Currently freestanding urban polyclinics (i.e., PHC facilities providing both primary and specialized outpatient services to the registered population) exist only in the capital city Yerevan and in the two largest cities of the country (i.e., Gyumri and Vanadzor).

Privatization in the health sector was also initiated in the mid-1990s and initially included the pharmacy network and most of the dental clinics in the country. An ad hoc privatization process took place in the first half of the 2000s for a limited number of mainly Yerevan-based hospitals. Since the last decade, new private hospitals have been largely investor owned, not former public facilities. In 2018, around three-quarters of all health human resources were employed by publicly owned health facilities, which also contained more than two-thirds of the total hospital bed capacity in the country. Yet private hospitals account for 32% of overall hospital capacity and treat almost 40% of all inpatient cases. Private hospitals employ just a quarter of the medical workforce, which suggests relatively higher efficiency of resource utilization by the private sector (Table 3).

Table 3: Health Care Resources of Armenia by Ownership Status, 2018

Indicator	Total	Public		Private	
		No.	%	No.	%
Hospitals	124	88	71.0	36	29.0
Hospital beds ('000)	12.2	8.3	68.0	3.9	32.0
Admitted hospital patients	406,393	245,364	60.4	161,029	39.6
Primary health care facilities	501	374	74.7	127	25.3
Medical doctors (all specialties)	13,366	9,981	74.7	3,385	25.3
Nurses and other mid-level medical staff	16,595	12,511	75.4	4,084	24.6

Source: National Institute of Health, Ministry of Health of the Republic of Armenia. 2019. *Statistical Yearbook: Health and Health Care.* Yerevan.

The underlying nuts and bolts of Armenia's current health financing were created in 1997 when the first BBP was introduced, line item budgeting was changed to purchasing of services, and all providers were contracted and allowed to charge formal user fees for noncovered services. Concomitantly in 1997, SHA was established as the independent public body charged with the task of purchasing all publicly funded inpatient and outpatient services in the country. It started operating in 1998, but in 2002 it was subordinated to MOH. In 2011, additional functions were transferred to MOH resulting in SHAs' loss of its independent status, which precluded it from operating like a freestanding insurer or purchasing entity. Since then, SHA only prepares the contracts with the providers, processes the reporting and disbursement of funds from the budget, and conducts audits. All major purchasing decisions are made by MOH, including selection of the providers to be contracted for service provision under the BBP, authorization of the contracts and verification of payments through the MOF's Client Treasury system. Thus, currently MOH acts as the sole purchaser of budget-funded medical services covered under the BBP by contracting and financing both public and private providers through SHA.

The complex nature of the BBP is at the heart of both the strengths and fundamental obstacles of Armenia's health system in achieving universal health coverage (UHC). Among its strengths are its focus on public and maternal health, emergency services, dread and catastrophic diseases, and needy populations. Its weaknesses lie in underfunding, limited financial protection and lack of coverage for personal health services for half the population, lack of modern incentive-based payment and referral arrangements, and out-of-date treatment protocols and practice guidelines.

Currently, the public budget contains five State Targeted Health Programs (STHPs) funding all services and benefits covered by the overall BBP. One of these STHPs focuses on the 19 State Order eligibility groups. The important and diverse policy elements embodied in specific public health and personal health benefits, eligibility criteria, and financing elements preclude consumer understanding, and ready assessment of impacts of eligibility and benefit changes, promote complexity in the development of public policy reforms in health financing, and result in significant administrative costs.

Given the exceedingly complex and narrowly targeted benefit and eligibility criteria, an estimated 50% of the population is not covered for comprehensive inpatient, outpatient, and diagnostic personal health benefits. Moreover, low payment rates for those covered as socially vulnerable groups precludes effective access and results in under-the-table payments, which further denigrates financial protection. Limited benefits for some services, such as outpatient drugs and complex diagnostic tests, result in significant OOP costs for most of the population.

Financing of the BBP is relatively straightforward as covered services are funded from the general government budget and copayments on some services for some groups, especially outpatient drugs. There are no earmarked payroll, income, value-added, or sin taxes or required premiums. Given the central role of the BBP in Armenia's public health financing system, it is worth providing a more detailed description of its basic underlying features as these highlight the areas of needed UHC policy reform options.

A major component of the health financing reforms in Armenia has been the introduction of new provider payment mechanisms. Currently, the main payment method of PHC services is capitation, whereby PHC facilities receive a fixed annual amount for each enrolled patient (the system of population's open enrollment with PHC providers was introduced in 2005). Per capita rates are differentiated for children and adults, and by geographical location (higher rates are applied for mountainous regions to cover higher maintenance costs of PHC facilities).

To improve the quality of PHC services and to increase the motivation of PHC providers to achieve certain performance and quality targets, performance-based financing indicators were introduced in 2010. The initial set of 10 indicators was later expanded to 30, and has been revised periodically every 2–3 years. However, the problem of ensuring adequate financial incentives for PHC providers to perform better is still not fully addressed. Due to limited public funding, the share of the performance-based financing component in the total income of PHC providers remains very low at around 3%.

Hospital services are paid on a fee-per-case basis where an average price is set for each completed surgical or nonsurgical hospital treatment case. Fee-for-service is used for the remuneration of both outpatient and inpatient providers for some specific types of services, such as diagnostic tests and procedures, ambulance services, provision of outpatient medicine to special categories of patients, and high-cost medical devices used in certain types of surgical operations. There are also other provider payment methods used to pay for a limited scope of services, such as the remuneration of fixed and variable costs for tuberculosis and psychiatric services, or the combination of case-based payment with bed per day per diems. Since 2011, copayments were introduced for certain categories of BBP services, which were aimed to cover the existing gap between the actual cost of the service and the BBP remuneration rate. The scope and rate of copayments are periodically revised.

CHAPTER III

Description of the Government-Funded Health Programs

The health policy priorities of the government are described in the annual State Targeted Health Programs (STHP), which are prepared by the Ministry of Health (MOH). After preliminary approval by the government, these are presented to the National Assembly of Armenia as part of the draft state budget message. There have been five programs included in the STHPs since its initial implementation in 1997 and until 2019:

- provision of primary health care (PHC) for the population;
- provision of medical care and services for individuals, included in socially vulnerable and other (special) categories of population;
- medical care and services for diseases that have social dependence and special significance;
- provision of maternal and child health care; and
- provision of hygienic and anti-epidemic safety of the population.

In developing an actuarial costing model for UHC reforms one needs to assess the BBP in terms of specific health financing policy levers, which include eligibility, benefits, financing— spending/revenues, provider payment, and any related delivery system or stewardship issues. For cost estimation and modeling purposes, one must create relatively homogenous benefit and eligibility groups amenable to modeling based on the available budget and State Health Agency (SHA) insurance claims information. For the modeling exercise, the Basic Benefit Package (BBP) programs were mapped into seven major groups:

- Catastrophic and Other Individual programs (based on a mix of social vulnerability and medical condition criteria);
- Outpatient Drugs;
- PHC, Outpatient, Emergency Care, Vertical Programs for Hospital Care;
- Public Health Services;
- Services Only for Vulnerable, Special Groups, and Women;

- Social Package; and
- State Order.

Similarly, in terms of eligibility expansions, the following groupings, which are available from the demographic and insurance data, are used for model costing purposes:

- Children;
- Disabled;
- Everyone Else;
- Formal Sector;
- Others in State Order;
- Pensioners; and
- Women's Programs.

This chapter will discuss the eligibility, benefits, financing sources, provider payment procedures, and delivery system for each group.

A. Primary Health Care, Outpatient, Emergency Care, Vertical Programs for Hospital Care

1. Eligibility Groups

All Armenians are eligible.

2. Benefit Categories

The benefits in this group, as they appears in the government budget, include

- emergency medical services for hospital services;
- embulance services;
- forensic and genetic services;
- global Fund-supported grant program on assisting the National human immunodeficiency virus/ acquired immunodeficiency syndrome (HIV/AIDS) Program in Armenia;
- Global Fund-supported grant program on strengthening the prevention of the tuberculosis in Armenia;
- HIV/AIDS prevention and care services;
- laboratory at the PHC level (such as blood tests, urine test, ultrasound, x-ray);
- medical care services for intestinal and other infectious diseases;
- medical care services for patients with drug and mental health disorders;
- medical care services for sexually transmitted diseases;
- medical care services of oncology and hematology diseases;
- medical services for diseases requiring continuous control and separate diseases;
- narrow specialized medical services at the PHC level;
- pathogenic services;
- primary health care such as visits to PHC doctors and gynecologist;
- sports medicine and anti-doping control services;
- tuberculosis medical care services; and
- tuberculosis, maternal and child health and family planning/ and reproductive health outcomes in Armenia grant program.

3.   Financing Sources

These services are mostly funded by the government from general revenues. The Global Fund also provides support for diseases such as tuberculosis and HIV/AIDS. A small portion is financed from OOP payments. While most services are provided free of charge, a few services, like medical care services for sexually transmitted diseases, oncology and hematology diseases, may require copayment for nondisabled and non-vulnerable populations, based on a price list issued by MOH.

4.   Provider Payment Procedures

PHC facilities are paid through capitation and a performance-based bonus system. Hospitals are paid per case, except for tuberculosis and mental health services, which are financed through a combination of fixed and variable cost reimbursement.

5.   Delivery System

Referral from PHC doctors is needed for the consultations with narrow specialists and laboratory tests. For vertical programs provided in hospitals, referral slips from PHC facilities are also needed. These PHC centers and hospitals are contracted by SHA.

B.   Public Health Services

1.   Eligibility Groups

All Armenians are eligible. The public awareness campaign for healthy nutrition is targeted only to school-age children.

2.   Benefit Categories

The benefits in this group, as they appears in the government budget, include

- blood collection services,
- healthy nutrition for children public awareness services,
- hygienic and epidemiological expertise services,
- national Immunization Program service support grant,
- national Immunization Program,
- promotion of healthy lifestyles and public awareness-raising services,
- services ensuring the sanitary and epidemiological safety of the population and public health services, and
- services for the disinfection of infectious diseases centers.

3.   Financing Sources

These services are mostly funded by the government from general revenues. The Gavi, the Vaccine Alliance also provides a grant for immunizations.

4.   Provider Payment Procedures

Public health services are provided as vertical programs with line item budgets.

5.   Delivery System

These are mostly vertical programs. These services are provided through the National Center for Disease Control and Prevention, as well as in PHC centers and hospitals that are contracted by SHA.

C.   Catastrophic and Other Individual Programs (Based on a Mix of Social Vulnerability and Medical Condition Criteria)

1.   Eligibility Groups

In principle, all Armenians are eligible, with priority given to disabled and vulnerable categories. For heart surgery services, only the following are eligible: Family Benefit Scheme recipients with poverty score of 36 and above, children from 0–7, and children from 7–18 who belong to one of the categories of the socially vulnerable population. For the non-vulnerable population, patients can write to the Minister of Health to appeal for coverage. When approved, patients can be treated without any charges. Facility global budget appeals are usually limited to 10% of the annual budget of facilities.

2.   Benefit Categories

The benefits in this group, as they appears in the government budget, include

- compensation of the travel cost of the patients referred to abroad for the treatment,[20]
- heart surgery services,
- hemodialysis services, and
- medical services with reproductive auxiliary technologies for infertile couples.

3.   Financing Sources

These services are mostly funded by the government from general revenues. When facility budget adjustment appeals are not approved, or the allocations of facilities are exhausted, patients must pay out-of-pocket.

4.   Provider Payment Procedures

Hospitals are paid per case for these services. Travel costs of patients referred abroad are paid for by MOH.

5.   Delivery System

Referral from PHC doctors is needed for the consultations for the narrow specialists and laboratory tests. For vertical programs provided in hospitals, referral slips from PHC facilities are also needed.

---

[20]   This benefit was discontinued after 2016.

D.   Social Package

In January 2012, a package of social benefits for public and civil servants was introduced, which included mandatory health insurance. The beneficiaries of the Social Package, irrespective of their job positions and salary have access to the Social Package services. The package does not only cover health benefits, it also provides monthly redemption of mortgage credits, tuition fees at accredited universities, and vacations in Armenia. This study focuses on health insurance, and the related services covered in the package.

1.   Eligibility Groups

Civil servants, public school teachers, and some other categories of public employees are eligible. A civil servant has an option to include his or her family in the package but must pay a premium.[21]

2.   Benefit Categories

See Appendix 1.

3.   Financing Sources

The program is funded by the government from general revenues.

4.   Provider Payment Procedures

Hospitals are paid per case. During 2012–2014, when the Social Package program was managed by private insurers, the total cost of the Social Package per beneficiary was AMD132,000 per year, from which AMD52,000 was the annual premium for the basic package of health insurance coverage. During 2014–2016, when the Social Package program was managed by SHA, there were no premium amounts fixed because the health component of the Social Package was included in the state health budget as one of the budget programs, from which hospital claims were paid by SHA, similar to other State Order programs (the average actual cost per beneficiary during this period was reduced to around AMD33,000).

Since 2017, when the implementation of the Social Package was again transferred back to the private insurers, MOH contracts with each of the six private insurance companies. These companies are involved in the program implementation as third-party administrators, based on the number of beneficiaries randomly allocated to each company, and the annual premium per beneficiary is calculated by dividing the available public budget funding for the program by the total number of Social Package beneficiaries at the beginning of the year. Private insurers take certain financial risks if actual claims exceed the allocated budget funds; however, they make a profit by retaining the surplus funding from MOH after the claims are settled.

---

[21]   A civil servant has an option to spend the rest of his or her Social Package benefit allocation for (i) an additional personal benefits package through private insurers (i.e., a supplementary insurance for non-covered benefits), or (ii) to cover a dependent family member, again through private insurers. The total annual sum of the Social Package allocation per beneficiary is AMD72,000.

5.   Delivery System

In 2014–2016, these services were provided in hospitals that are contracted by SHA. From 2017 onwards, these are provided in hospitals contracted by private insurers.

E.   State Order

Inpatient treatment covering more than 200 services (often aggregated) are provided with no copayment for selected poor, vulnerable, or special groups.

1.   Eligibility Groups

The Republic of Armenia (ARM) Government Decree No 318-N of 4 March 2004 regulates eligibility to include

- arrested, detained, and sentenced people;
- asylum seekers and their family members;
- beneficiaries included in the Family Benefit Scheme with a vulnerability score of 30.01 and above;[22]
- children left without parental care between 18 and 23 years of age;
- children under 18 years of age;[23]
- discharged people due to mutilation, injury, and disease during the military service who have not been recognized as disabled (hospital medical care and service within the individual rehabilitation program prepared by competent government authority in the area of medical and social examination);[24]
- military service personnel and their equivalents, members of their families, military service personnel who died (passed away) while defending the country, as well as during the discharge of official duties, former service personnel who are recipients of military pension for long years of service or disability;
- oppressed people;
- participants of the activities for elimination of trash in Chernobyl nuclear power plant;
- participants of the Second World War and their equivalents;
- people subjected to human trafficking;
- people under care in orphanages, retirement homes, and temporary shelters for the homeless;
- persons in the first disability group;
- persons in the second disability group;
- persons in the third disability group;
- persons of conscription age (hospital care and specialists);
- persons undergoing additional medical examination based on the referral notes of the competent government authority in the area of medical and social expertise;
- rescue service personnel and their family members, rescue service personnel relieved due to being on pension, members of families of rescue servants who passed away; and
- women of reproductive age during the pregnancy, delivery, and post delivery period.

---

[22]   In April 2020 this threshold was lowered to 28.01 by the Government.

[23]   In the baseline year (2016), only children younger than 7 years of age were eligible for State Order. In 2019, this was expanded to all children younger than 18 years.

[24]   This is the list of BBP beneficiary categories as of December 2019.

2.   Benefit Categories

See Appendix 1.

3.   Financing Sources

Government budget pays for all the services in State Order.

4.   Provider Payment Procedures

Hospital are paid based on cases they treated. Other services, such as outpatient diagnostic tests, are paid a fee-for-service.

5.   Delivery System

These services are provided in PHC centers, outpatient diagnostic centers, and hospitals that are contracted by SHA.

F.   Outpatient Drugs

1.   Eligibility Groups

These include disabled, vulnerable, and special categories of the population with different copayment rates (see below), as well as patients with certain health conditions and diseases.

2.   Benefit Categories

The benefit included in this group, as it appears in the government budget, is provision of medicine to individuals receiving outpatient, hospital care, and individuals included in special groups.

3.   Financing Sources

These services are mostly funded by the government from general revenues. A portion is financed from copayments, with the following breakdown: Medicine provided by the PHC facilities, which is procured and funded from their PHC per capita budget:

(a)   Eligible to Receive Free Drugs (i.e., 100% cost coverage by state budget)

- Children of families with disabilities (up to 18 years of age);
- Children of large families (aged 4-18 years);
- Children up to 7 years of age;
- Children without parental care, as well as one-parent orphans (up to 18 years);
- Disabled children (up to 18 years of age);
- Family members of service personnel killed during the defense of Armenia, as well as during their official duties;
- Participants in the Great Patriotic War[25] and their equals; and
- Persons with disabilities of groups 1 and 2.

---

[25]   Also called World War II

(b) Eligible to Receive the Drugs with 50% Copayment

- Chernobyl accident elimination participants;
- Children of single mothers (up to 18 years of age);
- Families consisting solely of nonworking pensioners (including children under their care);
- Oppressed;
- Pensioners who do not work and live alone; and
- Persons with disabilities of group 3.

(c) Eligible to Receive the Drugs with 30% Copayment

- Unemployed pensioners.

4.   Diseases and Conditions

Medicines are provided through the PHC facilities for patients with the following diseases and health conditions. The medicines are centrally procured by MOH and funded from a special public budget program.

(a) Chronic renal failure (in cases of renal transplantation and/or programmed hemodialysis) (cyclosporine, erythropoietin, mofetil mycophenolate and/or their equivalent);

(b) Epilepsy (anticonvulsants);

(c) Heart valve defects (anticoagulants after prosthesis);

(d) Malaria (antimalarial drugs);

(e) Malignant tumors (anti-cancer drugs, painkillers, narcotic drugs);

(f) Mental Illnesses (psychotropic drugs);

(g) Myocardial infarction (drugs to improve coronary blood circulation);

(h) Periodic disease (Familial Mediterranean Fever) (colchicine and/or other equivalent medicines);

(i) Phenylketonuria (baby food without phenylalanine);

(j) Tuberculosis (anti-tuberculosis drugs); and

(k) Type I and II diabetes (antidiabetic drugs).

5.   Provider Payment Procedures

Centrally procured drugs by MOH are provided in-kind through the PHC network, other drugs (for social categories) are reimbursed based on actual expenditures (fee-for-service) as part of the capitation rate of PHC budget.

6.   Delivery System

Drugs are provided through PHC facilities.

CHAPTER IV

Armenia's Current Health Financing Policy Priorities

According to the medium-term expenditure framework (MTEF) 2020–2022, the main goals of the government's health sector policies are the improved affordability and quality of health services and improved health status of the population.[26] While emphasizing the main strategic directions of the health policy in line with the State Targeted Health Programs (STHPs), the document further describes certain specific activities such as improving oncology and organ transplantation services, which are among the main targets of the Ministry of Health (MOH) for 2020–2022. The MTEF states that achieving these goals will depend greatly on the level of the health sector's public funding. Therefore, the health sector should be considered a public spending priority, with public budget allocations to the sector growing faster than overall budget expenditures. The MTEF then provides the projected 2020–2022 budget funding for the health sector, which suggests a 16.3% year-to-year increase in 2020, compared to the originally approved 2019 health budget, followed by a further 7.6% increase for 2021 and 9.6% for 2022.

However, in terms of the share of the health budget in total government spending, these indicators do not support the government's declared commitment to increased prioritization of the health sector. The health budget share decrease during 2020–2022, from the current 6% (adjusted mid-year 2019 budget) to 5.65% in 2022 (Table 4).

Detailed MTEF projections and the approved 2020 budget indicators for each of the 12 state budget programs are provided in Appendix 2.

A key MOH policy initiative related to the health financing reforms in Armenia, which is not reflected in the MTEF, is the proposal for the introduction of a universal health insurance (UHI) system in the country. Starting late in 2018, MOH has developed a draft concept note of the program, which was shared for public access and debate on 22 November 2019.[27] The new scheme aims to cover the formally employed population through a 6% earmarked payroll health tax, while the existing

---

[26] Medium-Term Expenditure Framework 2020–2022. Approved by the Government of Armenia (ARM), Decree No. 900-N on 10 July 2019.

[27] Available at https://www.e-draft.am/projects/2137 (in Armenian).

Table 4: Armenia State Budget Expenditures and the Health Budget (2016–2018 [actual], 2019 [approved and adjusted] and 2020–2022 [MTEF]) (AMD million)

Year	State Budget Expenditures (AMD)	Health Sector Budget (AMD)	Health Sector Budget as Share of the State Budget (%)
2016	1,449,063.6	88,645.9	6.12
2017	1,504,802.2	83,215.4	5.53
2018	1,447,083.0	79,574.2	5.50
2019 (approved)	1,648,063.1	89,590.0	5.44
2019 (adjusted*)	1,736,849.7	104,182.4	6.00
2020	1,871,676.7	107,213.3	5.73
2021	2,027,746.0	115,287.3	5.69
2022	2,235,466.7	126,350.3	5.65

AMD = Armenian dram.
Source: Ministry of Finance. https://minfin.am/ (as of 1 December 2019).

Basic Benefit Package (BBP) beneficiaries will continue to be covered by public budget allocations, which, however, will be transformed from current direct service payments to providers to insurance premium payments to the proposed single-payer public agency (the UHI Fund). Thus, the health risks of both employer-insured and publicly covered beneficiaries will be pooled under the centralized and publicly managed health insurance fund. The proposal suggests implementation of more unified benefits packages for different categories of beneficiaries, improved remuneration rates and payment mechanisms for the providers, and ability for the UHI Fund to exercise selective contracting of providers based on service quality assessments.

These reforms, if successfully implemented, can lead to better access and quality of care for the insured population and can result in more effective and efficient use of public resources by the health sector. MOH plans to start implementing the new insurance system in 2021, pending approval of the UHI concept paper by the government and adoption of the UHI Law and related legislative package by the National Assembly. However, the current coronavirus disease (COVID-19) pandemic is impacting these pre-COVID-19 decisions.

CHAPTER V

Basic Design Features for Actuarial Model

A. Simple Linear Actuarial Model

This chapter describes the Simple Linear Actuarial Model (SLAM), which has been programmed in Microsoft Excel and Visual Basic for Applications.[28] This approach assumes that the model prediction (in this report, the health expenditure) depends on both policy and demographic predictors, which include age, eligibility group, etc., which are the model inputs. Linear actuarial models, such as generalized linear models,[29] have been in use since the 1980s in developed countries to actuarially estimate required insurance premiums.[30]

SLAM extrapolates past historical utilization patterns of homogenous, mutually exclusive groups of individuals, and projects their health events and costs into the future based on regression. The advantages of this microlevel model is that it is flexible, transparent, and well-suited to study the short- to medium-term effects of alternative policy scenarios, such as changes in benefit packages, changes in enrollment criteria, changes in health utilization, changes in eligibility group demographics, and changes in health costs. It permits what-if scenario analyses and sensitivity analyses. The SLAM also provides estimates of health expenditures—and thus also the implied revenue needs or required actuarial premiums—by predefined eligibility groups and for different benefit packages.

Guerard et al. (2011) mention the difficulties in estimating the cost of providing health insurance cover to previously uncovered individuals.[31] Using their non-exhaustive list of key issues and factors for estimating the total health expenditures, Table 5 shows how these issues are tackled in this report and the actuarial model.

---

[28] Using Microsoft Excel and the programming language Visual Basic for Applications, which is commonly included in Microsoft Excel, assures that the program is available for all, as long as the user has access to a computer with Windows installed.

[29] The SLAM is a simple linear model, which assumes that the model prediction (in this report, the health expenditure) depends on the predictors (age, eligibility group, etc., which are the model inputs in this report). These predictors should also be modeled and estimated. In generalized linear models, these predictors are assumed to have a random component, which is assumed to be a distribution of the exponential family. While the predictors are estimated as well, the relation between the model prediction and model predictors is still assumed to be a linear function. See, for instance, M. Goldburd et al. 2016. *Generalized Linear Models for Insurance Rating*. Virginia: Casualty Actuarial Society.

[30] See, for instance, E. Ohlsson and B. Johansson. 2010. *Non-Life Insurance Pricing with Generalized Linear Models*. Heidelberg: Springer.

[31] Y. Guerard et al. 2011. *Actuarial Costing of Universal Health Insurance Coverage in Indonesia: Options and Preliminary Results (English)*. Washington, DC: World Bank.

Table 5: General Assumptions Actuarial Model

Factor or Issue	Assumption
Key demographic, socioeconomic, policy, and behavioral factors	
Socioeconomic and epidemiological status of covered and previously uncovered individuals	Input to the model Data source is SHA administrative and claims data All assumed constant
Benefit package, including scope, limits on benefits, and cost-sharing requirements	Input to the model Data source is SHA administrative and claims data Benefit packages are defined in the model, based on current Social Package and State Order BBP, and concept note as well as additional current benefits to special needs/vulnerable subgroups
Current service use	Input to the model Data source is SHA administrative and claims data Unless otherwise noted, assumed constant over the projection period
Demand effects or behavioral response to lower out-of-pocket costs for both current insureds and the previously uninsured	Input to the model Data source is SHA administrative and claims data Assumed no demand effects or behavioral response, unless otherwise specified as utilization bump for previously uninsured
Supply-side response (will supply expand sufficiently to meet newly created demand for health services?)	Not modeled Sufficient supply (e.g., infinite elasticity of supply) assumed
Cost containment or provider payment methods and levels, and ability of providers to extra-bill	Cost containment and/or provider payment methods are not modeled In some scenarios, price of State Order is harmonized with price of Social Package
Key issues for future program costs	
Demand for services	Input to the model Data source is SHA administrative and claims data
Increase in population	Input to the model Data are UN Census Data
Aging and epidemiological changes	Input to the model Data are from UN Census Data Population growth is modeled but epidemiological status is assumed constant (i.e., underlying epidemiology and/or medical practices do not change; change is only due to age-sex structure)
Delivery model	Not modeled
Technology adoption	Not modeled
Control of the use of medicines	Not modeled Outpatient drugs are included, but the model is indifferent on control of pharmaceutical use
Changes in the supply of primary care physicians, specialists, beds, laboratories and radiology facilities	Not modeled
Improvements in the quality of services and in efficiency	Not modeled

BBP = Basic Benefit Package, SHA = State Health Agency, UN = United Nations.
Source: Y. Guerard et al. 2011. *Actuarial Costing of Universal Health Insurance Coverage in Indonesia: Options and Preliminary Results (English)*. Washington, DC: World Bank. http://documents.worldbank.org/curated/en/685921468039053176/Actuarial-costing-of-universal-health-insurance-coveragein- Indonesia-options-and-preliminary-results.

Table 5 also shows that a number of variables are input assumptions in the actuarial model. These variables include health event costs for the first period, which are based on the claims information and the health event incidences for each eligibility group.[32] Demographics and growth of the eligibility groups over time period are also inputs to the model.

The unit of observation of the SLAM is the disaggregated age and sex cohort per eligibility group. However, the model input for SLAM is based on the State Health Agency (SHA) administrative data and claims data for State Order and Social Package eligibles, both of which provide data at the case level (i.e., the health events). Further assumptions are therefore needed with regard to demographic data and health utilization of individuals not covered under the Social Package or State Order. In the next sections these assumptions are further detailed.

The actuarial model only shows the public health expenditures under the benefit packages for both the current public Basic Benefit Package (BBP) and the proposed public universal health insurance (UHI) program in addition to the essentially existing budget costs for universally available public health, emergency services, primary care, dread diseases etc., services included in the BBP.[33] The formula of the simple linear model per eligibility group is

$$_g^b BBPHealthExpenditure_t = \sum_{g_h} \sum_{b_s} \left({}^b EventCost_t^{b_s} \times CostInflation_t \right) \times {}_{g_h} EventFrequency_t^{b_s}$$
$$\times \left({}_{g_h} Pop_{t=1} \times {}_{g_h} PopGrowth_t \times Enrol_t^{b_s} \right)$$

where

with output variables

$_g^b BBPHealthExpenditure_t$: the health expenditure in period t for eligibility group g and benefit package b

with input variables b

$^b EventCost_{t=1}^{b_s}$: the cost of health event s, under benefit package b, in period 1

$CostInflation_t$: inflation of health event costs in period t

$_{g_h} EventFrequency_t^{b_s}$: the frequency of health event s, under benefit package b, in period t of sex and age cohort h of eligibility group g

$_{g_h} Pop_{t=1}$: population of age and sex cohort h of eligibility group g in period 1

$_{g_h} PopGrowth_t$: population growth of age and sex cohort h of eligibility group g in period t

$_g^b Enrol_t$: enrollment factor of eligibility group g to be covered for benefit package b, in period t—in this report 1 or 0 (i.e., either the eligibility group is covered or not).

---

[32]   Health event incidences can be changed per period in the model. For this report, the incidences are kept constant unless otherwise noted.

[33]   The source of the revenues to finance these interventions determines whether they are public and/or private health expenditures. For example, if the benefit package were to cover all known health events but be financed fully from public funds, then the estimated health expenditure would equal the total public health expenditures. Conversely, if the financing source is OOP payment and private voluntary health insurance (PVHI), then the total would be total private health spending. As Armenia has always focused on UHI through a publicly financed system and given the very limited role of PVHI, the model focuses on total public spending per the approach outlined in the concept note. If PVHI and OOP-based claims data became available, one could modify the model for separate projections of public and private spending. One could also handle private spending through macro assumptions.

Public health expenditure, as presented in this report, is derived from

$$PublicHealthExpenditure_t = \sum_b \sum_g \left[{}^b_g BBPHealthExpenditure_t \right] + A + B$$

where

with output variables

$PublicHealthExpenditure_t$: health expenditures under the benefit packages, administration, and budget costs for the universally available services in period t with input variables

A: administration and capital expenditure expenses such as expenditures of ministerial staff at executive, state, and territorial governance bodies, medical equipment, construction of health facilities, among others

B: budget costs for the universally available services that are not for expansion, such as primary health care (PHC), outpatient, and emergency care, public health, catastrophic and other individual programs, as well as existing services available only for vulnerable, special groups, and women.

The actual expenditures for both A and B in 2016 are projected to 2021 using inflation data (see Assumption 2).

Assumptions provide model-specific details based on the same outline and discussion as given in the Model Use Manual. Assumptions in this report are only specific to the data or model for Armenia UHI.[34]

1.   General Assumptions

(a) Assumption 1: Number of Periods

The SLAM permits defining different periods (e.g., months, quarters, and years) to be used in the number of periods of projections. For this study, annual projections are made from 2016–2031. Only projections through 2021 are discussed in the report in detail, as they are most policy-relevant vis-à-vis the concept note, provide more robust estimates, and are less prone to accumulated projection errors and vagaries in the UHI specifications.[35]

(b) Assumption 2: Inflation for Expenditures

The inflation for expenditures ideally corresponds to the health sector-specific inflation rate, but in the absence of a reliable projection for health care inflation, we used the overall consumer price index (CPI). The International Monetary Fund's (IMF) October 2019 prediction of the overall CPI inflation factor (Table 6) has been utilized in the model. Sensitivity analyses were performed using health-specific inflation factors as well as more recent, but highly uncertain, 2020 post-pandemic revised growth estimates from the Asian Development Bank (ADB) and the IMF.

---

[34] For more details please see ADB. 2020. *Manual on the Simple Linear Actuarial Model.* Manila.
[35] The underlying projection factors for the model have been provided for a 15-year projection period (2016–2031). Projections until 2031 are provided in the micro model spreadsheets.

Table 6: Inflation Variables

Year	Consumer Price Index (%)
2017	0.92
2018	2.52
2019	2.12
2020	3.00
2021	3.18

Source: International Monetary Fund. 2019. *World Economic Outlook.*

(c) Assumption 3: Data for Incidences

Data for the actuarial model were obtained from SHA database for 2016 Social Package and State Order (inpatient services). Both programs include different population groups, usually categorized by age group, marital status, employment status, disability, and military service. Due to changes in the administration of the Social Package, which had been transferred to private health insurers as third-party administrators, and due to data completeness issues of claims data due to the transition to the e-health system in 2017, it was decided that the 2016 claims data are currently the most complete and most reliable. The 2016 SHA claims data and membership data are both available for the Social Package and for the State Order.[36] In Assumption 19, the differences in how health services are defined under the Social Package versus under the State Order are further explained. Assumptions 20 and 23 detail respectively how the health frequencies and health costs are derived from SHA claims data.

Private health insurance data are not included. Despite multiple requests by the ADB to private health insurers to obtain health utilization data on their private sector members, these data were not shared. Also not included are the out-of-pocket (OOP) payments at public and private hospitals. There is no record of these OOP payments in either SHA health records or in the e-health system. Before 2017, as the hospitals did not have to submit claims for any of these costs to the government, these visits were not reported or accounted for. Even after the e-health system became operational in June 2017, no law was passed to make it mandatory for hospitals to record their OOP paid visits, and these data are therefore still missing.

Confronted with missing health utilization data for all Armenians not covered under the Social Package or the State Order (about 50% of the population), assumptions had to be made regarding their health services frequencies and costs. Prices are assumed to follow either the State Order or Social Package costs, depending on the scenario. Health utilization is extrapolated using the available SHA data either based on Social Package or State Order data, depending on eligibility.

This means that it is assumed that private and pre-UHI uninsured people will have the same epidemiological traits and health utilization patterns as their demographically equivalent (by age and sex) SHA covered counterparts—a rather strong assumption. Data on this group should be collected in the future so that this assumption can be changed in future iterations of the model. Given the sensitivity of the results to the utilization information, it would be advisable in the

---

[36] Had they been available, it would be advisable to use the average incidences of multiple years of utilization data, which in turn would allow us to obtain more robust model estimates.

future to use the average incidences of multiple years of utilization data, which in turn would allow more robust model estimates.

For the health services that currently cover everyone, such as PHC, outpatient, and emergency care, public health, catastrophic and other individual programs, current incidence is assumed to remain constant.

(d) Assumption 4: Data for Outpatient Drugs

Expenditure for outpatient drugs was estimated from the Integrated Living Conditions Survey (ILCS 2016) dataset.[37] ILCS data include questions relevant to outpatient drugs expenditure for everyone in the survey, and it also provides their age, gender, employment status, and social category. For details, see Appendix 1.

(e) Assumption 5: Health Utilization Bump: Increased Utilization Due to Unmet Need

Data from ILCS were used to project the impact of UHI on patients who had previously forgone care because of lack of access or affordability. Utilization of health services is assumed to increase once UHI is introduced proportionate to the respondents with unmet demand, estimated to be around 17%. Details on how this was derived are provided in Appendix 1. At the launch of UHI, utilization increases drastically, after which it will normalize, but to a higher level than pre-UHI levels.

(f) Assumptions 6: Administrative Costs

Administrative costs are assumed to remain stable over the various scenarios, increasing only with inflation over the years. Information regarding actual administrative and/or management needs of the purchasing agency are unavailable.[38] This assumption should be revised in future simulations. Given that coverage will increase by approximately 50%, there will likely be consequential implications for administration costs.

2.   Covered Population and Eligibility Assumptions

(a) Assumption 7: Covered Population

The covered population refers to the population intended to be covered by the health insurance programs, i.e., the whole population of Armenia. The model input is based on SHA administrative data and claims data, which only include data on those covered by the Social Package or State Order benefit packages. Administrative data from SHA only includes the number of people registered in each eligibility group for 2018. This includes the covered population with and without utilization in 2018. The 2018 numbers per eligibility group were projected back to 2016—the year for which the claims data were complete—based on United Nations Statistics Division (UNSTAT) population data projections.[39] However, the

---

[37] Statistical Committee of the Republic of Armenia. 2018. *Integrated Living Conditions Survey 2017 microdata set.* https://www. armstat.am/en/?nid=205 (accessed 3 January 2020). The question includes both over the counter and prescription medicines and will most probably overestimate expenditures (*ceteris paribus*).

[38] While administration expenses could be obtained, they do not reflect the expected funding needs of a real purchasing agency. It can readily be expanded to accommodate other policy reforms in terms of eligibility groups, BBPs, revenue sources, provider payment/purchasing policies, and other delivery system and governance reforms.

[39] Except for pensioners, where data available is from 2016.

administrative data do not include information on the age and sex of the insured per eligibility group. Therefore, the population breakdown in terms of age and sex groups was assumed to be similar to the overall population.[40]

Data from UNSTAT are also utilized for the demographic projections. Since the UN provides data by age-sex for 5-year intervals, constant absolute change is assumed between intervals to estimate the population growth rates for each age-sex cohort. Finally, assumptions were also needed on the demographic data of individuals not covered under the Social Package or State Order, which were based on the UNSTAT data after subtracting the eligibility groups covered by the Social Package or State Order benefit packages. Details on how adjustments were made are provided in Appendix 1.

(b) Assumption 8: Eligibility Groups

There are currently 19 different eligibility groups in the State Order and the civil servants for Social Package. These groups were subsumed into six more aggregate eligibility groups as shown in Table 10 to make it easier to present in the model.

(c) Assumption 9: Eligibility Group—Children

All children younger than 18 years of age are in this category, regardless of whether there are cases within this age cohort in the Social Package or State Order. For calculating the incidences, and fully accounting for all the services availed by the children, data for all those aged 0–17 years from the State Order were appended. Children were divided into three age cohorts: 0–1, 2–7, and 8–17 years of age. The government previously covered children aged 0–7 years, and it now plans to cover all those younger than 18 years. Therefore, the aforementioned age groupings allow the model to cover that additional group by separating out children aged 8–17 years. More importantly, complete claims data are available for children aged 0-7 years. However, data for those aged 8–17 years were only available for a small group because the majority were not covered under children's services. The third age cohort (0–1 years of age) has been separated due to the generally higher cost of children in that age group, thus allowing examination of the expenditure estimates for that age cohort.

(d) Assumption 10: Eligibility Group—Formal Sector

This group includes those aged 18–63 employed in the formal sector. All individuals aged 18–63 years and in the Social Package are divided into six cohorts of age-sex: males and females (aged 18–24, 25–44, and 45–63 years). Those younger than 18 years and older than 63 years are excluded from the Social Package database. Thus, the adult eligibility groups breakdown used these three age cohorts: 18–24, 25–44, and 45–63 years of age; and these are also the age cohorts used for all other adult eligibility groups in the model. Adults aged 18–24 years are also the ones who can be classified as students in colleges or universities; hence it allows the government to separately estimate expenditures for students by using this age group.

Cases are gathered based on the services in the Social Package, and for each service full price is assumed to be covered (100% reimbursement is applied for calculating the expenditure). A consequence of having one eligibility group for the public and private formal sectors is that

---

[40] See Appendix 1 for a more detailed explanation.

the eligibility group (albeit disaggregated by sex and age cohort) is assumed to be homogenous. As available claims data only cover the public sector, this means that it is assumed that the health utilization of the formal private sector (once covered and excluding a possible utilization bump) is similar to the health utilization of the public sector members. Data collection on health utilization trends for the private health sector in the UHI will help to validate or correct this assumption, based on which the SLAM can be updated.

(e) Assumption 11: Eligibility Group—Disabled

Using the State Order dataset, the disability group has been defined as the those aged 18–63 years who that fall in disability groups 1, 2, or 3 as defined by the State Order. As with other adult eligibility groups (e.g., formal sector), the disability group is also divided into three age cohorts: 18–24, 25–44, and 45–63 years of age.

(f) Assumption 12: Eligibility Group—Pensioners

Similar to the children's eligibility group, pensioners are also defined solely based on age. Sixty-three is the retirement age for both men and women in Armenia; hence, those older than 63 years are included in the pensioners' category. For calculating the incidences, and fully accounting for all the services availed by the pensioners, data for all those aged above 63 from Social Package and State Order were appended. Pensioners were divided into three age cohorts: 64–69, 70–74, and 75+ years of age. Armenia has an aging population, with the highest growth in the pensioners cohort; therefore, dividing into multiple groups aids in future decision-making related to strategic purchasing.

(g) Assumption 13: Eligibility Group—Others in State Order

This group includes those individuals from the State Order data who do not fall into the disability category and are not children or pensioners. They are divided into three age cohorts like the formal sector and disabled: 18–24, 25–44, and 45–63 years of age.

(h) Assumption 14: Eligibility Group—Everyone Else

Finally, the last category everyone else includes the population between 18–63 years of age who are not covered in Social Package or State Order in 2016. These are the individuals who are paying all their inpatient health services through OOP payments and/or possibly private health insurance, and there is no record of them in SHA health records or in the e-health system.

Before 2017, these visits were not reported or accounted for as the hospitals did not have to submit claims for any of these costs to the government. Even after the e-health system became operational in June 2017, no law was passed to make it mandatory to record their OOP paid visits; hence, these data are still missing. This residual eligibility group therefore includes the informal sector (which includes the self-employed and underemployed population), those working in the agricultural sector, and students aged 18 years and above, among others. Data on health utilization of this group is unavailable in any of the administrative data. For modeling purposes, the health utilization is assumed to be similar to that of formal sector, following their age-sex breakdown of 18–24, 25–44, and 45–63 years of age.

(i)   Assumption 15: Mutually Exclusive Eligibility Groups

Members of eligibility groups are assumed to be mutually exclusive. That means an individual cannot be in two or more groups simultaneously. This also implies that we need to consider which group takes precedence over the other.

(j)   Assumption 16: Eligibility Groups' Order of Precedence

If an individual falls into multiple eligibility groups, keeping the groups mutually exclusive requires a decision regarding which group takes precedence. Given that the eligibility group criteria for children or pensioners are based solely on age, they can therefore not fall into another category. Similarly, the disabled group takes precedence over all other adult eligibility groups (ages 18–63 years) due to its more generous package and defined eligibility criteria.[41] The formal sector, others in State Order, and everyone else are already mutually exclusive; therefore precedence is not considered here.

Based on this order of precedence, the share of each eligibility group in the population is shown in Table 7.

Table 7: Projected Percentage Share of Eligibility Groups, 2016–2021
(%)

Year	Total	Children	Formal Sector	Disabled	Pensioners	Others in State Order	Everyone Else
2016	100	23.27	24.04	4.40	12.15	6.28	29.87
2017	100	23.31	23.90	4.40	12.45	6.24	29.69
2018	100	23.36	23.76	4.40	12.75	6.21	29.52
2019	100	23.40	23.62	4.41	13.06	6.17	29.34
2020	100	23.45	23.45	4.41	13.37	6.13	29.17
2021	100	23.30	23.33	4.37	13.92	6.10	28.98

Source: United Nations Department of Economic and Social Affairs. 2019. *World Population Prospects*. https://population.un.org/wpp/Download/Standard/Population/.

The total population per eligibility group is shown on Table 8.

Table 8: Projected Population per Eligibility Groups, 2016–2021
(No.)

Year	Total	Children	Formal Sector	Disabled	Pensioners	Others in State Order	Everyone Else
2016	2,997,974	697,528	720,753	131,905	364,266	188,312	895,441
2017	2,985,562	695,970	713,556	131,408	371,696	186,432	886,500
2018	2,972,874	694,368	706,359	130,911	379,127	184,551	877,558
2019	2,960,140	692,718	699,162	130,415	386,558	182,671	868,617
2020	2,947,355	691,018	691,165	129,918	393,989	180,790	859,675
2021	2,946,140	686,305	687,330	128,781	410,228	179,579	853,917

Source: United Nations Department of Economic and Social Affairs. 2019. *World Population Prospects*. https://population.un.org/wpp/Download/Standard/Population/.

---

[41]   It is assumed in the concept note that in UHI, no one will be worse off than before the UHI.

3.   Population and Growth Rates

(a)   Assumption 17: Generating Populations within Age Groups

Age cohorts are defined specific to each eligibility group. All eligibility groups have three age cohorts each: children aged 0–1, 2–7, and 8–17 years; (ii) pensioners aged 64–69, 70–74, 75+ years; and (iii) all other eligibility groups aged 18–24, 25–44, and 45–63. Since these age cohorts differ from the population cohorts provided in the UN database, further adjustments were done to generate the required age cohorts[42] (Table 9).

Table 9: Formation of Age Cohorts for the Actuarial Model Based on United Nations Age Cohorts

UNSTAT Age Cohort (years)	Age Cohort in the Actuarial Model (years)	Eligibility Group
0–4	0–1	Children
5–9	2–7	
10–14	8–17	
15–19		
20–24	18–24	Formal sector, disabled, others in State Order, everyone else
25–29	25–44	
30–34		
35–39		
40–44		
45–49	45–63	
50–54		
55–59		
60–64		
65–69	64–69	Pensioners
70–74	70–74	
75–79	75+	
80–84		
85–89		
90–94		
95–99		
100+		

UNSTAT = United Nations Statistics Division.

Source: United Nations Department of Economic and Social Affairs. 2019. *World Population Prospects.* https://population.un.org/wpp/Download/Standard/Population/.

---

[42]   See Appendix 1 for details on adjustments.

(b) Assumption 18: Growth Rates of Subpopulations

Growth rates are defined by using the UNSTAT 5-year intervals data. For each 5-year interval, constant absolute change in population per year is calculated, and then growth rates are generated based on that change. Appendix 3 shows the tables on population growth rates.

4.   Health Services

(a) Assumption 19: Health Services

The State Order benefit package has defined 200 health services, while the Social Package has defined 407 health services.[43] Given that eligibility groups under State Order and Social Package are mutually exclusive, the model made use of all 200 health services for State Order, and all 407 health services for Social Package. A full list of health services is available in Appendix 1.

5.   Event Frequency (Prevalence and Incidence)

(a) Assumption 20: Event Frequency

Event frequency for the Social Package or State Order is calculated using existing claims data based on the formula

$$_{g_h}EventFrequency_t^{b_s} = \frac{_{g_h}Events_t^{b_s}}{_{g_h}N_t}$$

where

$_{g_h}EventFrequency_t^{b_s}$: the frequency of health event s, under benefit package b, in period t of sex and age cohort h of eligibility group g, and $g \in \{Social\ Package,\ State\ Order\}$

$_{g_h}Events_t^{b_s}$: number of occurrences of health event s, under benefit package b, in period t of sex and age cohort h of eligibility group g, and $g \in \{Social\ Package,\ State\ Order\}$

$_{g_h}N_t$: number of individuals of sex and age cohort h of eligibility group g in period t, and $g \in \{Social\ Package,\ State\ Order\}$

The number of events (i.e., cases) is divided by the number of covered persons in the cohort, which includes the persons with cases and without cases (see Assumption 7 on how the age and sex cohorts were constructed).

For Armenians who were not covered pre-UHI, it is assumed that their health utilizations are similar to that of persons of the same sex and age cohort who are covered pre-UHI. It is assumed frequencies stay constant over time:

$$_{q_h}EventFrequency_t^{b_s} \equiv {}_{g_h}EventFrequency_t^{b_s} \qquad \forall\ t$$

---

[43]   The SLAM also defines groupings of health services, called health categories, for example for inpatient and outpatient services. For this report the health categories are not relevant and are not discussed further.

where

$_{q_h}EventFrequency_t^{b_s}$: the frequency of health event s, under benefit package b, in period t of sex and age cohort h of eligibility group, and $q \in \{Social\ Package,\ State\ Order\}$

$_{g_h}EventFrequency_t^{b_s}$: the frequency of health event s, under benefit package b, in period of sex and age cohort h of eligibility group g of sex and age cohort h, and $g \in \{Social\ Package,\ State\ Order\}$

6. Benefit Packages and Reimbursement Rates

(a) Assumption 21: Benefit Packages

For UHI scenarios, the State Order for children is expanded cover to all those younger than 18 years (as the policy took effect in July 2019). In the pre-UHI 2016 baseline, State Order cover was only for children aged 0–7 years. For pensioners, only disabled pensioners are covered in the pre-UHI 2016 baseline, but for UHI scenarios, they are covered by services from both State Order (if disabled) and Social Package for all other pensioners. Disabled and others in State Order groups are provided with the services in the State Order that they had been previously covered for. In pre-UHI 2016, only civil servants are provided with Social Package, while the military are provided with State Order Package. In UHI scenarios, the military keeps the State Order Package, civil servants keep their Social Package, and the rest of the Formal Sector employees are modeled to receive the Social Package as well. In the pre-UHI 2016 baseline, the everyone else group has no coverage. In the UHI scenarios, this formerly uncovered group, which includes the informal sector, self-employed, agriculture workers, among others, is modeled to receive the Social Package.

(b) Assumption 22: Heterogeneity of Benefit Packages

In hospital services, both programs—Social Package and State Order—reimburse for their procedures separately. For example, in addition to whatever service is performed, in both packages, magnetic resonance imaging and computed tomography scan are reported separately. This means that a patient on a single visit, with the same primary diagnosis and ICD-10 codes, could have more than one service provided. Furthermore, services are defined differently in both programs. The Social Package has 407 services, and State Order has 200 services. However, it could not be clearly assumed that either one provides more services than the other as Social Package defines services more narrowly, while State Order defines them more broadly. For example, in the Social Package, neurosurgery has several service categories, but in State Order it only has one. There is no clear mapping between Social Package and State Order services. For the purposes of this study, services from both packages have been used, which provides us a more detailed model as incidences are calculated for each service in each package. However, no cross-program mapping was done. Instead, they were used as inputs to the model separately.

(c) Assumption 23: Reimbursement Rates

Prices are taken from MOH-approved reimbursement rate list for 2016 State Order and Social Package services.[44] Full reimbursement is assumed for both programs without any copayments.

---

[44] The model is based on the average current public spending under the existing programs. The model then attributes these averages

As Social Package reimbursement rates are higher than State Order rates, for the introduction of UHI, prices for State Order programs were increased to match the prices of Social Package program. The average price of the Social Package is ~2.3 times that of the State Order program (details on calculation are provided in Appendix 1). Unfortunately, due to lack of any 1-1 mapping methodology, this simplistic generalizable measure was used to increase the prices of the State Order to harmonize with the Social Package. An analysis that maps the different services in the State Order and Social Package should be performed to more accurately derive the impact of price harmonization.

Table 10 summarizes the important assumptions used in the model.

Table 10: Summary of Modeled Population Covered and Assumptions

Eligibility Group	Covered Population (No.)	Age Cohorts (years)	Program Expanded	Assumption (group-specific)
Children	697,528	0–1 2–7 8–17	• State Order • Outpatient Drugs	• All aged <18 years • Population number from UNSTAT
Formal Sector	720,753	18–24 25–44 45–63	• Social Package (civil servants and all other formal employees) • State Order (military) • Outpatient Drugs	• 53% of working population aged 18–63 years; formal sector percentage from Armstat • Military continues to have State Order
Disabled	131,674	18–24 25–44 45–63	• State Order • Outpatient Drugs	• Aged 18–63 years • Numbers from Ministry of Labor and Social Affairs • Aggregated Disabled groups I, II, III
Pensioners	364,266	64–69 70–74 75+	• State Order (if disabled) • Social Package (if employed) • Outpatient Drugs	• All aged >63 years • Population number from UNSTAT
Others in State Order	188,312	18–24 25–44 45–63	• State Order • Outpatient Drugs	• Numbers from State Order that are not disabled and aged 18–63 years
Everyone Else	895,441	18–24 25–44 45–63	• Social Package • Outpatient Drugs	• Deducting all the above numbers from total population

UNSTAT = United Nations Statistics Division.
Source: https://population.un.org/wpp/Download/Standard/Population/

to newly covered individuals. The model can be used to model alternative average cost per person scenarios but the place to start for micro claims models of this type is with the current baseline system. Once the model parameters are calibrated against the actual baseline data and total public health spending, one can simulate the costs of alternative coverage and pricing policies.

B.   Model Validation

SLAM estimates are validated against actual expenditures for State Order and Social Package eligibles in 2016. Actual expenditures for the State Order are derived by adding the budget lines of the following: medical services for socially vulnerable and special groups, children's medical care services, medical care services for military service men and their family members, and hospital care services and examination for military and pre-military individuals. For Social Package beneficiaries, expenditures are derived from the line-item medical care services for employees of the state institutions and organizations. The difference between the estimated and actual expenditures for the two different groups are marginal, accounting for 1% for State Order, and 0.05% for Social Package (Table 11). Based on these results, the estimates from SLAM are assumed to be valid.[45]

Table 11: Actual vis-à-vis Estimated Expenditures from the Actuarial Model

Item	Actual Expenditure in 2016 (AMD '000)	Estimated Expenditure from SLAM (AMD '000)	Difference (No.)	Difference (%)
State Order	17,774,872.9	17,580,438.5	194,434.4	1.09
Social Package	2,644,436.9	2,643,075.0	1,361.9	0.05

Source: Ministry of Health of Armenia, 2016 Budget; Estimates from the Manual on the Simple Linear Actuarial Model (SLAM).

C.   Operationalization of the Model

To model the projected Armenian UHC costs, the SLAM is used to estimate future costs for both the Social Package and State Order, while macro-adjustments are made to services such as public health, emergency, and dread disease that are already available to the whole population in 2016. The SLAM provided per capita estimates of expenditures for children, formal sector, disabled, pensioners, others in State Order, and everyone else, for 2016 and 2021. To arrive at total expenditures, these per capita amounts are then multiplied by the 2016 population and the 2021 projected population by eligibility groups and benefit category. Behavioral assumptions are included in some scenarios, such as the harmonization of State Order prices to that of Social Package, and the increase in utilization due to unmet need for previously uncovered individuals.

For the services that currently cover everyone, such as PHC, outpatient and emergency care, public health, catastrophic and other individual programs, as well as existing services available only for vulnerable, special groups, women, administrative and capital expenditures, actual expenditure in 2016 is simply projected to 2021 using inflation and demographic changes. The expenditure items are mapped according to Armenia's MOH budget and distributed to their respective eligibility groups (see Appendix 4). These services refer to the items that are considered as constant (i.e., already included in the 2016 baseline for the currently covered population) in the calculation.

Figures used for MOH actual expenditure for 2016 came from the executed budget, based on MOH official data. Projected budget data for 2021 used came from MTEF 2020–2022 figures. GDP figures for 2016 came from MTEF 2019–2021, while the figure for 2021 came from MTEF 2020–2022.

---

[45]   This error rate embodies the imputations done on demographic data from UNSTAT and number of eligible population from 2018 SHA administrative data.

CHAPTER VI

Results

The model is a flexible tool that can evaluate numerous health financing policy options implemented over various time periods. The actuarial modeling of future public health expenditures is based on (i) the health utilization and health utilization trends; (ii) the benefit packages (i.e., health services that are covered, including whether there are copayments required);[46] (iii) the demographics of the currently insured population and assumptions regarding enrollment of new groups, timing, and their demographics; (iv) assumptions regarding population growth; and (v) the cost of health services and cost trends. Combining these leads to the actuarial estimates of health expenditures (Figure 10). Changes in expenditures from the pre-universal health insurance (UHI) baseline inform policymakers of future incremental and total expenditures and revenue needs. Table 12 illustrates five scenarios.

Figure 10: Policy Options Available for Simulation in the Model

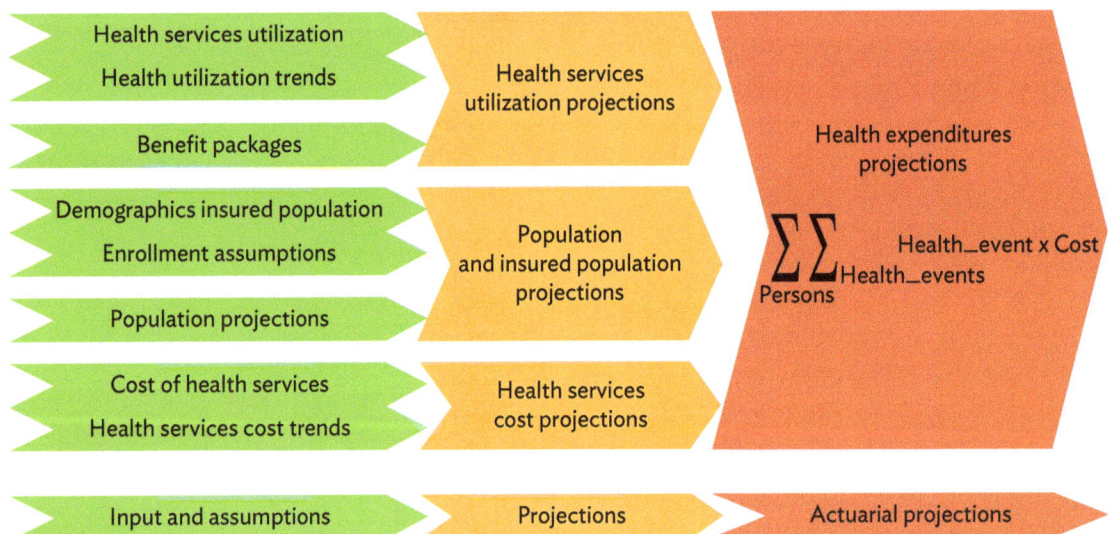

Source: Authors.

---

[46] While the model can simulate cost-sharing provisions, given the lack of cost-sharing detail in the concept note, the estimates including drugs, assume full UHI reimbursement, resulting in an overstatement of the costs to the program of government-financed drugs and other services requiring cost-sharing.

Table 12: Modeled Scenarios

Eligibility Group	UHC Dimension	Scenario 1	Scenario 1a	Scenario 2	Scenario 3	Scenario 4
Year		2016	2016	2016	2021	2021
Children						
	Coverage	Children 0–7 years old	Children 0–7 years old	Children below 18 years old; utilization bump after UHI introduction for newly covered children aged 8–17 years	Children 0–7 years old	Children below 18 years old; utilization bump after UHI introduction for newly covered children aged 8–17 years
	Width (benefit)	State Order	State Order	State Order and outpatient drugs	State Order	State Order and outpatient drugs
	Depth (price)	Non-harmonized	Harmonized	Harmonized	Harmonized	Harmonized
Formal						
	Coverage	Military; civil servants	Military; civil servants	All formal	Military; civil servants	All formal in 2021
	Width (benefit)	State Order for military; Social Package for civil servants	State Order for military; Social Package for civil servants	State Order for military; Social Package for civil servants and all other formal and outpatient drugs; utilization bump after UHI introduction for newly covered formal employees	State Order for military; Social Package for civil servants	State Order for military; Social Package for civil servants and all other formal and outpatient drugs; utilization bump after UHI introduction for newly covered formal employees
	Depth (price)	Non-harmonized	Harmonized	Harmonized	Harmonized	Harmonized
Pensioner						
	Coverage	Not covered	Not covered	All aged 64+ years covered; utilization bump after UHI introduction for newly covered pensioner	Not covered	All above 63 years covered in 2021; utilization bump after UHI introduction for newly covered pensioner

continued on next page

Table 12 *continued*

Eligibility Group	UHC Dimension	Scenario 1	Scenario 1a	Scenario 2	Scenario 3	Scenario 4
	Width (benefit)	Not covered	Not covered	Social Package and outpatient drugs	Not covered	Social Package and outpatient drugs
	Depth (price)	Not covered	Not covered	Harmonized	Not covered	Harmonized
Disabled						
	Coverage	Covered	Covered	Covered	Covered	Covered
	Width (benefit)	State Order	State Order	State Order and outpatient drugs	State Order	State Order and outpatient drugs
	Depth (price)	Non-harmonized	Harmonized	Harmonized	Harmonized	Harmonized
State Order–Others						
	Coverage	Covered	Covered	Covered	Covered	Covered
	Width (benefit)	State Order	State Order	State Order and outpatient drugs	State Order	State Order and outpatient drugs
	Depth (price)	Non-harmonized	Harmonized	Harmonized	Harmonized	Harmonized
Everyone Else						
	Coverage	Not covered	Not covered	Everyone else covered; utilization bump after UHI introduction	Not covered	Everyone else covered in 2021; utilization bump after UHI introduction
	Width (benefit)	Not covered	Not covered	Social Package and outpatient drugs	Not covered	Social Package and outpatient drugs
	Depth (price)	Not covered	Not covered	Harmonized	Not covered	Harmonized

UHC = universal health coverage, UHI = universal health insurance.
Source: Authors.

For model development and/or validation and policy relevancy purposes, five scenarios were simulated. For 2016, three scenarios were developed: two relate to the pre-UHI baseline being compared at differing reimbursements rates, and one assesses the costs in 2016, if UHI had been fully implemented that year, including increases in utilization resulting from unmet need.

The pre-UHI baseline is scenarios 1 and 1a. Scenario 1 is the actual 2016 pre-UHI baseline of no UHI and different payment rates for State Order and Social Package beneficiaries; and Scenario 1a, which is otherwise the same as Scenario 1, evaluates what 2016 costs would have been if State Order payment rates were raised to Social Package payment levels. Scenario 1 is used to validate and calibrate the model by adjusting the parameters to assure estimates equate to the actual State Health Agency (SHA) claims information as well as all government spending on health as reported in annual budget documents. Scenario 1a provides a useful order of magnitude estimate of the policy to raise State Order payment rates to the Social Package levels, this policy being a precursor to UHI, albeit not in place in 2016.

Scenario 2 assumes full implementation of UHI in 2016. It shows what the costs of the UHI proposal would have been if it had been fully implemented in 2016. This provides a useful validation for the proposed concept note 2021 implementation date estimate as it abstracts from projection errors from the 2016 base as well as possible changes in spending estimates due to demographic, socioeconomic, and macroeconomic factors including uncertainties in the 2020 and 2021 macroeconomic projections resulting from the coronavirus disease (COVID-19) pandemic currently impacting Armenia and the rest of the world.

It is a simple but useful validation on the magnitude of the future projections, and provides a good, *ceteris paribus*, comparison for the 2016 pre-UHI baseline. In addition, this scenario adjusts for harmonized Social Package and State Order payment rates as well as the utilization bump resulting from meeting the unmet need of previously uninsured individuals.[47] Unmet need was estimated from the 2016 Integrated Living Conditions Survey, which suggested a 17% increase in utilization (and hence the expenditure) for those newly covered. The utilization bump was estimated as a sum of those who could not afford treatment (5.7%), those who did not think the problem was serious enough (9.2%), those with a doctor friend or relative (1.3%), or any other reason due to which they were ill but did not see a doctor (0.6%).

Scenario 3 is simply the pre-UHI baseline Scenario 1a projected out to 2021. The pre-UHI baseline projections are inclusive of the equalized payment rates as those additional costs are already budgeted in the medium-term expenditure framework (MTEF) and are therefore part of the 2021 pre-UHI baseline spending. Thus, they should not be considered as an incremental cost of UHI in 2021.

Scenario 4 assumes full UHI implementation in 2021 as proposed in the concept note,[48] which includes the utilization bump.[49] This scenario provides estimates of the total costs and revenue needs in 2021 and the derived incremental costs of implementing UHI in 2021. Since the more immediate shorter-term costs are of most interest, for policy purposes, only the 2016 and 2021 results are presented here, while model projections are made through 2031. Given the uncertainties and significant changes in the 2020 and, to a lesser extent, the 2021 macroeconomic growth and health inflation estimates resulting from the COVID-19 pandemic, we provide UHI estimates based on the pre-pandemic growth estimates, and perform a sensitivity analysis using the April 2020 pandemic influenced International Monetary Fund (IMF) growth projections.[50] Table 13 summarizes the scenarios.

---

[47]   For illustration purposes, the 17% utilization bump was applied only in 2016 for Scenario 2. This will manifest over a number of years.

[48]   Given that the model assumes that the changes for 2016–2021 are only inflation and population growth, UHI expansion in 2016 has been projected out to 2021, which is Scenario 4.

[49]   For illustration purposes, the 17% utilization bump was applied only in 2021 for Scenario 4. This will manifest over a number of years.

[50]   The May 2020 *IMF Republic of Armenia Second Review Under the Stand-By Arrangement Program* uses the same annual CPI inflation factors as the April 2020 WEO except for a 0.1 percentage point difference in the 2020 CPI (0.8% in the April WEO vs 0.9% in the May program document). As the differences in terms of the estimated UHI cost estimates are trivial, the IMF's April 2020 WEO results are presented in the sensitivity analysis.

Table 13: Main Features of Modeled Scenarios

Scenario	Main Features
1: Pre-UHI Baseline Scenario with Different Pricing	Based on the 2016 situation (no UHI) Separate State Order and Social Package pricing
1a: Pre-UHI Baseline Scenario with Harmonized Pricing	Based on the 2016 situation (no UHI) Harmonized Social Package pricing levels (i.e., State Order pricing at the same level as Social Package pricing)
2: UHI Introduced In 2016	UHI applied to 2016 Harmonized Social Package pricing levels Utilization bump for previously uninsured
3: Pre-UHI 2021 Projection with Harmonized Pricing	No UHI Harmonized Social Package pricing levels
4: UHI Introduced In 2021 With Harmonized Prices	UHI introduced in 2021 Harmonized Social Package price levels Utilization bump for previously uninsured

UHI = universal health insurance.

Given the lack of UHI Basic Benefit Package (BBP) specificity in the existing government policy documents, it is assumed that for non-vulnerable and nonspecial needs groups (e.g., private formal sector workers) the UHI BBP is the Social Package BBP. For groups who fit into the 2016 special needs or vulnerable categories and are eligible for additional services, it is assumed that those groups will still be covered for their additional group benefits that were covered in 2016. In other words, everyone is covered either *de minimis* by the Social Package BBP and/or their more extensive 2016 vulnerability subgroup BBP.

While the model at present does not have a dedicated revenue module, it provides information about the additional resources that will be needed to fully fund UHI. It also shows additional expenditures and funding needs disaggregated by eligibility groups and service categories. Therefore, it provides useful guidance to policymakers about possible revenue enhancement policies in terms of new or existing general (e.g., income, payroll, property, value added tax, excise taxes) and earmarked taxes, voluntary or mandatory individual premiums and/or cost-sharing. Moreover, a critically important policy outcome from expanding eligibility and benefits under UHI is that such expansions will reduce private out-of-pocket (OOP) costs significantly (currently about 8% of gross domestic product (GDP), over 80% of all health spending, and about 8% of all household spending). This considerably increases the ability to pay taxes and/or premiums for many non-vulnerable individuals, who are among the major beneficiaries of the public UHI expansion.[51]

Table 14 summarizes the results for the five scenarios in terms of spending levels by eligibility and benefit category for both the 2016 and the 2021 implementation scenarios. Overall public spending changes on health as a share of the budget and GDP are also shown. The two 2021 Scenarios (3 and 4) are based on the IMF's pre-COVID-19 October 2019 World Economic Outlook (WEO) overall inflation and growth projections. Table 15 shows sensitivity analysis using the current April 2020 WEO projected pandemic-influenced growth estimates as well as 2021 projections based on health-specific inflation factors. The differences in results are insignificant for the alternative inflation scenarios and use of health care as opposed to general inflation factors, heavily reflecting the IMF's current assumptions that in 2021 economic growth will likely bounce back to close to the pre-pandemic projected levels.

---

[51]   This resembles US Medicare Part B program, where beneficiaries can pay a subsidized voluntary premium for outpatient services not covered elsewhere in the program.

Table 14: Universal Health Insurance Scenario Expenditure Estimates

	Scenario 1	Scenario 1a	Scenario 2	Scenario 3	Scenario 4
	Pre-UHI Baseline Scenario with Different Pricing	Pre-UHI Baseline Scenario with Harmonized Pricing	UHI introduced in 2016	Pre-UHI 2021 Projection with Harmonized Pricing	UHI introduced in 2021
	FY2016	FY2016	FY2016	FY2021	FY2021
Item			(AMD million)		
PHC, OPD, EC, vertical hospital programs	33,261	33,261	33,261	35,810	35,810
Public health	4,851	4,890	4,851	5,225	5,225
Catastrophic and other individual programs[a]	5,736	5,736	5,736	6,175	6,175
Restricted services[b]	11,316	11,316	11,316	11,903	11,921
State Order	17,580	37,231	68,480	39,394	81,047
Social Package	2,643	2,643	38,058	2,685	40,666
Outpatient drugs	3,330	3,330	79,830	3,424	87,723[c]
Subtotal	**78,717**	**98,407**	**241,532**	**104,616**	**268,567**
Children	20,789	31,077	44,564	31,694	47,653
Formal sector	16,383	18,242	37,665	19,101	40,250
Disabled	6,031	9,718	17,789	10,444	19,329
Pensioners	7,159	8,350	60,110	10,888	74,347
Others in State Order	6,608	9,274	11,504	9,769	12,201
Everyone else	13,093	13,093	61,246	13,680	65,748
Women's programs	8,653	8,653	8,653	9,041	9,041
Subtotal	**78,716**	**98,407**	**241,531**	**104,617**	**268,569**
Administration and capital expenditure[d]	9,727	9,727	9,727	10,659	10,659
Modeled Total	**88,443**	**108,134**	**251,258**	**115,276**	**279,228**
Excess/(shortfall)	201			12	
Actual health budget	88,645			115,287	
Percent of budget	**6.12%**	**7.46%**	**17.34%**	**5.68%**	**13.77%**
Percent of GDP	**1.75%**	**2.13%**	**4.96%**	**1.51%**	**3.67%**

AMD = Armenian dram, EC = emergency care, FY = financial year (corresponds to the calendar year), GDP = gross domestic product, OPD = outpatient services, PHC = primary health care, UHI = universal health insurance.

Note: The two 2021 scenarios 3 and 4 are based on the pre-COVID-19 macro growth projections as presented in the October 2019 International Monetary Fund World Economic Outlook. These projections are redone using the revised current pandemic influenced April 2020 International Monetary Fund World Economic Outlook projections and are presented in Table 16. The changes in the model results are trivial as are changes in universal health insurance estimates also shown in Table 16 from using health sector specific as opposed to overall growth inflation factors.

[a] Eligibility based on a mix of social vulnerability and medical condition criteria.

[b] Services only for vulnerable.

[c] Based on ILCS 2017 if all the outpatient drugs expenditure is covered.

[d] This is constant and has only been adjusted by the inflation factor.

Source: Authors' calculation.

Table 15: Sensitivity Analysis: Universal Health Insurance Scenario Expenditure Estimates

	Health Inflation Armenia		ADB ADO April 2020		IMF WEO April 2020	
	Scenario 3	Scenario 4	Scenario 3	Scenario 4	Scenario 3	Scenario 4
	Pre-UHI 2021 Projection with Harmonized Pricing	UHI Introduced in 2021	Pre-UHI 2021 Projection with Harmonized Pricing	UHI Introduced in 2021	Pre-UHI 2021 Projection with Harmonized Pricing	UHI Introduced in 2021
	FY2021	FY2021	FY2021	FY2021	FY2021	FY2021
Item	(AMD million)					
PHC, OPD, EC, vertical hospital programs	34,487	34,487	35,691	35,691	34,894	34,894
Public Health	5,032	5,032	5,208	5,208	5,091	5,091
Catastrophic and other individual programs[a]	5,947	5,947	6,155	6,155	6,017	6,017
Restricted services[b]	11,463	11,481	11,863	11,882	11,598	11,617
State order	38,214	78,160	38,469	79,605	38,334	77,828
Social package	2,588	39,215	2,636	39,940	2,577	39,048
Outpatient drugs	3,297	84,481	3,412	87,432	3,336	85,480
Subtotal	**101,028**	**258,802**	**103,434**	**265,912**	**101,849**	**259,975**
Children	30,781	45,932	31,115	47,063	31,145	46,012
Formal sector	18,403	38,783	18,918	39,824	18,496	38,935
Disabled	10,067	18,624	10,308	19,164	10,078	18,736
Pensioners	10,491	71,644	10,794	73,611	10,553	71,968
Others in State Order	9,404	11,757	9,654	12,089	9,438	11,819
Everyone else	13,174	63,354	13,634	65,151	13,330	63,696
Women's programs	8,706	8,706	9,011	9,011	8,809	8,809
Subtotal	**101,028**	**258,802**	**103,434**	**265,912**	**101,849**	**259,975**
Administration and capital expenditure[c]	10,263	10,263	10,622	10,622	10,385	10,385
Modeled Total	**111,291**	**269,065**	**114,056**	**276,534**	**112,233**	**270,359**
Excess/(shortfall)	3,996		1,231		3,054	
Actual health budget	115,287		115,287		115,287	
Percent of budget	5.49	13.27	5.62	13.64	5.53	13.33
Percent of GDP	1.46	3.53	1.50	3.63	1.47	3.55

ADB = Asian Development Bank, ADO = *Asian Development Outlook*, AMD = Armenian dram, EC = emergency care, IMF = International Monetary Fund, FY = financial year (corresponds to the calendar year), GDP = gross domestic product, OPD = outpatient services, PHC = primary health care, UHI = universal health insurance, WEO = World Economic Outlook.

[a] Eligibility based on a mix of social vulnerability and medical condition criteria.

[b] Services only for vulnerable.

[c] This is constant, and has only been adjusted by the inflation factor.

Source: Authors' calculation.

Table 16: Inflation Rates for Sensitivity Analysis

Year	IMF Inflation (%)	Health Inflation (Provided by CBA) (%)	ADB ADO April 2020 (%)	IMF WEO April 2020 (%)
2017	0.92	2.63	1.00	1.00
2018	2.52	1.16	2.50	2.40
2019	2.12	(1.86)	1.40	1.40
2020	3.00	3.00	2.80	0.80
2021	3.18	3.18	2.20	2.00

( ) = negative, ADB = Asian Development Bank, ADO = *Asian Development Outlook*, CBA = Central Bank of Armenia, IMF = International Monetary Fund, WEO = World Economic Outlook.
Sources: International Monetary Fund. World Economic Outlook Databases. https://www.imf.org/external/pubs/ft/weo/2019/02/weodata/index.aspx (accessed 3 January 2020) and ADB. 2020. *Asian Development Outlook 2020: What Drives Innovation in Asia?* Manila. https://www.adb.org/sites/default/files/publication/575626/ado2020.pdf.

In 2016, actual budget expenditure amounted to AMD88 billion. If we assume that UHI is implemented fully in 2016 at harmonized prices, then this would cost an additional AMD163 billion, implying that government public health expenditure for implementation of UHI would increase public spending on health more than twofold to AMD251 billion. That would mean increasing health expenditure as share of GDP from 1.75% to 4.96%. The public health share of the budget will increase from 6.12% to 17.34% (Table 16).

In terms of expenditure category, inpatient expenditure (i.e., the sum of Social Package and State Order) has the highest cost at ~AMD106 billion, followed by outpatient drugs at ~AMD80 billion. It is important to note these are also the two service groups that are being expanded, while the rest continue with the same service coverage available to the entire population as before (PHC; catastrophic; and services specific to vulnerable, special, and women).

In terms of population groups, with UHI, the everyone else group has the highest expenditure at AMD61 billion, closely followed by the pensioners group at AMD60 billion. Expenditures of children below 18 years of age are AMD44 billion, formal sector AMD37 billion, disabled group is AMD18 billion, while others in State Order are at AMD11.5 billion. It is expected that women's programs will continue to be provided free to the whole population, and expected expenditure is AMD9 billion.

Inpatient expenditure in 2016 under UHI would cost AMD106 billion. Pre-UHI, it was at AMD20 billion—an increase of more than fivefold. Pensioners have highest per capita inpatient expenditure of AMD65,240, followed by the disabled group at AMD49,300[52] and children at AMD40,790.

---

[52] The relatively low amount for disabled group is an artifact of classifying disabled elderly under pensioner.

Outpatient drugs in 2016 cost ~AMD79 billion. Pensioners have the highest per capita outpatient drugs expenditure at AMD84,420, which is even higher than their per capita inpatient services expenditure. It implies that the old-age population is more likely to spend on outpatient drugs, which makes sense as they have highest probability of relying on continuous medication for chronic conditions. This group also includes the disabled aged above 63 years and that further pushes up the cost. In contrast, the children group has the least outpatient drugs expenditure, with lowest per capita at AMD4,660. It implies that children are the least likely to rely on outpatient medications as only children younger than 3 years are expected to get sick more often, and as they get older, especially for those aged 8–17 years, expenditure will fall drastically and hence reduce the overall expenditure of children for outpatient drugs.

For 2021, under full UHI with harmonized prices, Scenario 4, expenditure would amount to AMD279 billion. This is an increase of ~AMD191 billion if compared to the status quo (as per 2016 actual expenditure Scenario 1). That would also mean increasing health expenditure as a share of GDP from 1.75% to 3.67%. Health spending as a share of the budget will increase from 6.12% to 13.77%. In terms of expenditure category, inpatient expenditure (sum of Social Package and State Order) has the highest cost at ~AMD121 billion, followed by outpatient drugs at ~AMD88 billion. In terms of population groups, with UHI, pensioners at ~AMD74 billion has the highest expenditure, followed by everyone else at AMD66 billion.

Examining the future macroeconomic situation shows that health funding in the MTEF 2021 is not enough to cover the UHI implementation. Based on the MTEF, the health sector will be publicly funded with AMD115 billion in 2021. This will account for only 1.51% of GDP and is insufficient for UHI implementation. More specifically, inpatient services are allocated AMD61 billion in 2021 in the MTEF. For full implementation of UHI in 2021, inpatient expenditure allocation is estimated to be ~AMD121 billion;[53] therefore, the current allocation in MTEF needs to be doubled to cover the inpatient UHI. The total 2021 public health sector expenditure will need to more than doubled as well, from AMD115 billion to AMD279 billion for full UHI implementation.

From the fiscal and macro perspective, from 2000–2017, Armenia's nominal GDP per capita increased by more than fivefold from $622 in 2000 to almost $4,000 in 2017. In terms of the GDP growth rate, Armenia has made improvements since the 2009 recession, when the real GDP growth rate dropped to –14%. The IMF Article IV 2019 update as well as the IMF's May 2020 Republic of Armenia Second Review Under the Stand-By Arrangement project that Armenia's growth rate is expected to remain at 4%–5% from 2021–2024.[54] Since its recovery from recession, Armenia has not been able to attain the same level of growth as it previously had.

From 2000–2008, Armenia averaged a real GDP growth rate of more than 10%. Overall fiscal balances are expected to remain negative. General government expenditures as a percentage of GDP have decreased slightly from 27% in 2016 to 23% in 2018, but revenue as percentage of GDP has not changed much. Therefore, the IMF projects that fiscal balance as share of GDP will remain in the range

---

[53] Estimated from the actuarial model, assuming UHI goes into effect fully in 2021.
[54] IMF. 2019. Republic of Armenia: 2019 Article IV Consultation. *IMF Country Report.* No. 19/154. Washington, DC; and IMF. 2020. Republic of Armenia: Second Review Under the Stand-By Arrangement, Requests for Augmentation of Access, Modification of Performance Criteria, and Monetary Policy Consultation Clause-Press Release; Staff Report; Staff Supplement; and Statement by the Alternate Executive Director. *IMF Country Report.* No. 2020/176. Washington, DC.

of –2.5% to –1.5%. Options to create future fiscal space that will be needed for UHC implementation include: (i) increasing government revenues either through existing projected growth and/or through dedicated health taxes, (ii) reprioritizing health over other sectors in the budget, (iii) improving the efficiency of existing outlays, and perhaps most challenging is (iv) finding ways to capture as public revenues the large reductions in private OOP payments that UHI will create. Unfortunately, the current COVID-19 pandemic could be a short-term impediment to these efforts.

Armenia's total tax revenue as share of GDP remains significantly below most countries of the Organization for Economic Co-operation and Development (OECD) as well as other comparable income countries. Around 95% of all revenues come from taxes as Armenia is not a physical resource endowed country. Within taxes, the value-added tax accounts for 34.4% of all tax revenues, which is highest portion of the revenue. It is followed by the individual income tax, which accounts for 29% of total revenue. The corporate income tax accounts for 9.3% of total revenue. OECD countries on average have a 34% tax-to-GDP ratio. Armenia's tax-to-GDP ratio is around 20%, which shows there is still a significant margin for increasing revenue through various tax measures.

Recent research has also focused on ways to estimate the tax potentials of the country, and how much more tax can be collected. Based on revenue composition data for Armenia, estimates suggest that Armenia's tax potential (defined as tax-to-GDP ratio) is 41.8%, which is almost double the current tax-to-GDP ratio.[55] Armenia's tax-to-GDP ratio has risen slowly but consistently from around 14% in 2000 to 20% in 2017, but there remains significant potential revenue that can be generated through more optimal taxation policies. Earmarked taxes (e.g., tobacco and alcohol), taxes on formal sector workers and employers, tax subsidies to purchase public or private health insurance, mandated individual premiums, and cost-sharing are examples of potential mechanisms for increasing public revenues for health.

Sensitivity analysis using the current April 2020 ADB- and IMF-projected pandemic influenced growth rates shows that the difference between expenditure estimates are minor. All estimates suggest that for UHC with harmonized pricing would lead to a health budget of 13.27% to 13.77% of total government expenditure, and 3.53% to 3.67% of the GDP. The highest estimates are from the inflation factors used in the original modeled estimates, and the lowest are from using health consumer price index (CPI) inflation rate of Armenia instead of overall CPI. These different inflation rates show that total expenditure estimates for UHC will not differ much and will be around AMD275 billion in 2021. It is important to note that this is just a model, and estimates will change depending on the data being input. Given that COVID-19 has drastically changed the global economic situation and is having a major impact on Armenia's economy, it is hard to predict how much it will actually cost to implement UHC in 2021. That is also the reason we see lower estimates from recent IMF WEO inflation numbers (April 2020), because the inflation has been reduced for 2020 keeping in line with the economic impact of COVID-19 for Armenia.

Data description for sensitivity analysis. Sensitivity analyses were performed based on varying inflation rates. Four different inflation rate sources were used, and all provided Consumer Price Indexes with only minor differences. First is the CPI based on the IMF's most recent data as of (October 2019), when initial model simulations were performed. The second source provides CPI estimates based on

[55]   J. Mawejje and R.K. Sebudde. 2019. Tax revenue potential and effort: Worldwide estimates using a new dataset. *Economic Analysis and Policy*. (63): pp. 119–129. doi: 10.1016/j.eap.2019.05.005.

the health and medical-related basket of goods and services for Armenia. The third source utilizes ADB's most recent update based on its *Asian Development Outlook* publication, which provides ADB's most recent estimates for Armenia's inflation rate. Finally, the IMF's World Economic Outlook (April 2020) further adjusts the CPI based on the economic impact of the ongoing COVID-19 pandemic. The most recent update of ADB and IMF sources (ADO and WEO respectively) have minor differences in their estimates but, more importantly, their results do not differ significantly. ADO and WEO April 2020 are both very similar, except for the 2020 inflation estimate where IMF's estimates are much lower, accounting for the projected severe economic impact of COVID-19.

CHAPTER VII

Next Steps

This report assists in the development of an Armenian actuarial costing capacity to assess the total and incremental expenditures and revenues associated with alternative health financing (eligibility, benefit, purchasing, and derived revenue requirements) policies to achieve universal health insurance (UHI). It is an initial attempt to model a complex health financing system, which has evolved over the past 25 years from its former Soviet Union national health system roots in a somewhat ad hoc, rather than holistic, manner as incremental reforms were periodically adopted to modernize and improve various aspects of the system's performance. Armenia's health financing situation is somewhat unique for an upper middle-income country as over 86% of its health spending is private, over 80 percent of which, is from private out-of-pocket (OOP) household payments. Achieving universal health coverage (UHC), while improving health outcomes and financial protection, in the context of the country's available fiscal space and challenging demographics as well as the coronavirus disease (COVID-19) pandemic, is at the forefront of its current policy agenda. This concluding chapter of the report discusses next steps in refining and institutionalizing the model. In addition, it discusses Armenia's health financing and UHI efforts in a broader overall health reform context.

A.   Future Potential Model Refinements

1.   Short-Term Model Refinements

Once issues in data quality[56] in the e-health system have been resolved, the actuarial model should be re-estimated using the latest available e-health data for 2019. Modifying the utilization probabilities based on multiple years of utilization data should be assessed. Sensitivity analyses, particularly using different factors to harmonize State Order to Social Package prices, should be conducted. A short-term fix could involve comparing factors derived from average prices of smaller subsets of more comparable procedures in both the State Order and Social Package. Administrative cost should also be re-estimated to account for the significant increase in coverage as well as the likely impacts of alternative payment methodologies, quality measures, and gatekeeper or referral systems on administrative costs.

---

[56]   For example, data input of cases needs to be completed, errors in classification of cases rectified, and completeness of beneficiary data assessed.

2. Institutionalizing the Model

Simple Linear Actuarial Model (SLAM) is an easy-to-modify excel based model or program with a user manual (footnote 34). Training for an appropriate government unit should be provided to ensure institutionalization. Refinements to the expenditure projections, could better identify who benefits, their profiles, and their ability to pay. Knowing this will help in the design of financing options, particularly revenue-raising options.

3. Data Quality Improvements

The e-health system should collect information for all Armenians, and for all cases (inpatient, outpatient and PHC), not just those covered by the public BBP. Crucial information that is currently lacking include: public and private OOP payments, outpatient visits, and codes from the International Classification of Diseases, among others. A mapping of the health services of the Social Package to the State Order or vice-versa needs to be done to allow for proper harmonization of prices and benefits which will aid in standardization of benefit packages, payment definitions and reimbursement rates for the two programs. To be able to estimate implications of UHI on administration costs, actual needs of the purchasing agency should be estimated.

4. Revenue Module

SLAM can be expanded to include a revenue module that will include an analysis of the impacts of possible funding sources such as general tax, earmarked tax, external sources, and mandatory or voluntary premium payments, perhaps means-tested.

5. Cost of Health Services

The current model uses average reimbursement rates from the State Order pricing and the Social Package pricing as inputs for the cost of health services. A next step would be to use estimates of the normative or efficient costs of healthcare providers to provide health services. These cost estimates can be sourced from a costing study based on Armenian health facilities on local practices and clinical flowcharts specifying activities, including time spent by health personnel, services rendered, and drugs provided. With the highest OOP payment in the world, there is reason to believe that too low reimbursement rates are one of the causes of unofficial under-the-table payments. Using these estimated actual efficient costs of healthcare services provision would provide an idea of the actual, real, or efficient national cost of health care.

6. Strategic Purchasing of Services

Different strategies of purchasing of health services influence behavior of both healthcare providers as well as patients. Changing the relative prices of a normal delivery versus a caesarean section may reverse the upward trend of caesarean sections in Armenia, which increased from 7.2% in 2000 to 31.0% in 2017.[57] The actuarial model can indicate those services with the highest impact in terms of financing costs. Incorporating strategic purchasing assumptions regarding the impact of purchasing strategies on utilization would be an important next step in both model development and payment policy reform.

---

[57] M. Tadevosyan et al. 2019. Factors Contributing to Rapidly Increasing Caesarian Section in Armenia: A Partially Mixed Concurrent Quantitative-qualitative Equal Status Study. *BMC Pregnancy and Childbirth*. 19 (2). https://bmcpregnancychildbirth. biomedcentral.com/articles/10.1186/s12884-018-2158-6.

Table 17 summarizes weaknesses and recommends future steps.

Table 17: Data Weaknesses and Critical Assumptions

	Assumptions	Causes, Rationale, Problem Statement	Possible and/or Recommended Future Steps
Data Weaknesses			
1.	SHA numbers of beneficiaries for 2018 per BBP eligibility group are used to retrospectively estimate the size of the eligible groups in 2016.	Only the 2018 numbers of beneficiaries by eligibility group were provided; those for 2016 were not available, except for pensioners.	• There is no complete BBP beneficiary database by eligible groups. The data standards and quality of the database will therefore need to be improved up to international standards.
2.	The age and sex composition of beneficiaries in the BBP eligible groups are assumed to be similar to that of the general population.	The composition of the eligibility groups is not known.	• The model input can then be updated to obtain more accurate actuarial health expenditure estimates.
3.	SHA claims data on hospital services for individuals covered under the State Order and Social Package benefit packages for 2016 represent the general inpatient health services utilization of Armenian citizens.	The 2016 SHA claims data is considered the most complete claims data on health utilization because it contains data on reimbursed health services for both the Social Package and State Order.	• There is no complete and detailed health utilization database that accounts for outpatient, inpatient, PHC and referral health utilization. Data on patient characteristics (age, sex, eligibility group, location, etc.), health status (diagnoses), and health utilization (visits, follow-ups, drugs provided and prescribed, etc.) should be collected for multiple years, both for public and private providers.
4.	Because no health utilization data was available for PHC services, a lumpsum was used (and changed in line with the demographic and inflation projections).	For PHC services covered under the benefit packages, health care providers are paid on a per capita base, and do not submit patient-level health service utilization data to SHA.	• The model input can then be updated to obtain more accurate actuarial health expenditure estimates.
5.	Expenditure for outpatient drugs was estimated from the ILCS (2016) dataset. Moreover, outpatient drugs prescription is assumed to remain the same over the scenarios.	Little data is available regarding outpatient drugs provided. Centrally procured drugs by MOH are provided in-kind through the PHC network, other drugs (for social categories) are reimbursed based on actual expenditures (fee-for-service) as part of the capitation rate of PHC budget. There is a limited scope (width) of outpatient drugs coverage by the public budget for only certain social groups and people with certain diseases. Even for those groups, the actual level of drugs provision (depth of coverage) was never fully achieved due to different reasons (insufficient public funding, perceived low quality of publicly procured drugs, hence patients' unwillingness to accept them, etc.). So, if the future UHI scheme will promise free outpatient drugs to all covered, then it will have major cost implications.	• While the drugs on the Armenian Essential Medicines List are covered for certain vulnerable population groups, it is known that drugs are an important contributor to the OOP payments of the population at 38.7%. • Drugs prescription and drugs provision data should be collected in the health utilization database. • Once outpatient drug prescription can be linked to health services rendered, and costs for prescribed drugs can be better estimated, these can be used to update the actuarial model.

continued on next page

Table 17 *continued*

	Assumptions	Causes, Rationale, Problem Statement	Possible and/or Recommended Future Steps
	Critical Modeling Assumptions		
1	Price factor to bring State Order benefits up to Social Package price levels is assumed to be equal to the average price of Social Package is ~2.3 times that of State Order program	As there is no clear mapping between Social Package and State Order services, a simplistic factor based on the average price levels of each was used. (Note: Staring 1 July 2019, MOH has partially moved to utilizing the Social Package prices for reimbursement of State Order services, which can provide more accurate data for the next round of actuarial estimates.)	An analysis that maps the different services in State Order and Social Package should be performed to correctly derive the impact of price harmonization and allow for proper harmonization of prices and benefits. This will help standardize payment definitions and reimbursement rates for the two programs.
2.	The current 19 BBP eligibility groups are modeled into six eligibility groups.	There was little information of the size and composition of the eligibility groups.	If better beneficiary administrative data becomes available with clearer exclusive eligibility group attribution criteria, the actuarial model can be extended to differentiate between more eligibility groups.
3.	All predictors for the health expenditure are model input.	Given the scarcity and limited quality of the claims and beneficiary data, a Simple Linear Actuarial Model was used.	With more years of claims and enrollee data of a higher quality available, a more sophisticated generalized linear model can be envisioned to better estimate the average health expenditure per case (in case of fee-for-service payment systems) and per enrollee.

BBP = Basic Benefit Package, MOH = Ministry of Health, PHC = primary health care, OOP = out-of-pocket (payment), SHA = State Health Agency, UHI = universal health insurance.

[a] Nineteen different eligibility groups are based on social or employment status, which, when combined with certain medical conditions and the selective benefits within the different groups, result in dozens of unique eligibility and benefit category combinations.

Source: Authors.

B.   Policy Options Development for the Future

Health financing reform policies cannot be developed, analyzed, and implemented in a vacuum without taking into account the other interactive health system components of human capital, physical infrastructure, equipment and technology, pharmaceuticals and medical supplies, information systems, and governance and stewardship, as well as the full range of the social determinants of health, which also include areas such as long-term care and social services, areas of particular importance given Armenia's aging, migrating and declining population. Indeed, modern integrated care payment approaches are predicated on consumer centered networks that focus on coordinating health and social services. Indeed, one fallout of the COVID-19 epidemic is the need to assess health sector spending components in a holistic manner that considers both interaction within the health sector as well as between health and other critical health influencing sectors including social assistance, unemployment compensation, housing, water, etc. Such assessments will be increasingly critical in determining future fiscal space allocations and sector prioritization in the budget.

In addition, while this report has focused on the public sector, private spending and delivery are critical pillars of the health system. Current policy documents are rather vague about the role of private health insurance, which currently only accounts for about 1.2% of all health spending. Yet policies to support the purchase of private health insurance could well help offset public UHI spending.[58] On the other hand, without prohibitions on private health insurance policies covering public cost-sharing requirements, such complementary polices could result in increases in publicly insured spending as dually insured consumers facing zero price at the point of service will overconsume free public services.

Payment and BBP policies on extra-billing, have important implications for OOP payment, financial protection, equity, and overall cost control. In a similar vein, sufficient public and private delivery capacity is essential for the success of UHI in terms of access, quantities, quality, and spatial distribution. Understanding delivery system dynamics also has important implications for cost estimates, as supply response is one of the critical elements of all actuarial models, and one of many areas in which Armenia-specific behavioral response data are lacking.

While Armenia's Five-Year Development Plan and concept note refer to these other components of the health system, it is unclear what the concurrent processes are for holistically considering all these interrelated health system components and developing, analyzing, and costing proposed parallel reforms. Given the magnitude of the proposed public health spending increases and the COVID-19 pandemic, this will be particularly important.

One approach that has been used by many countries, somewhat similar to the internal MOH process used to develop the UHI concept note is to create a formal high-level interagency health reform task force to develop, analyze, cost, and then implement a broad array of health system reforms. Given the current major distraction from UHI reform as a result of the COVID-19 pandemic, once Armenia's pandemic response is fully under control, formal establishment of a health reform task force could help refocus public and government attention back on UHI as well as future pandemic preparedness. The health reform task force could be broken up into different working groups, each responsible for a different health system component. Depending on the complexity and size of the country and its health sector, there can be a handful of groups such as health financing, human resources for health, infrastructure, pharmaceuticals, information systems, among others.[59]

There should be a central costing capacity to assess the costs of each group's proposals and account for interaction effects. The working groups would report to a steering committee composed of senior officials from the relevant government agencies and outside stakeholders. If such an overall health reform approach is not advisable at the present time, the government might still want to consider a similar high-level transparent public process to resolve the contentious and unresolved UHI health financing issues inherent in the concept note proposal including revenue raising and a health tax, rationalizing and simplifying the BBP, developing specific performance-based, integrated care purchasing arrangements focused on efficiency and quality, and developing needed health management information systems, among others.

---

[58]   Private health insurance could help if it is complementary, covers most of the population, and is subsidized for poor.
[59]   In the 1990s, the Clinton Health Reform Task Force in the United States was composed of 24 groups, which took on every aspect of the health sector.

A public policy process focused on the costs, benefits, tradeoffs, and health reprioritization may assist in reconciling divergent views. This is also important in garnering public support for proposed health taxes and/or other revenue enhancements designed to capture and transfer reduced private OOP spending into public coffers. Indeed, while the expenditure projections show the large incremental public expenditures to implement UHI, it is also clear that many of the groups benefiting would be better-off formal private and informal sector workers, who currently are spending over 8% of their household budgets on health. The question is what the best options are to raise additional revenues for health to fund UHI, which are equitable, administrable, acceptable to the public, non-distortionary to the economy, assure financial protection, raise sufficient revenues, and are sustainable.

Are there some combinations of changes in existing taxes,[60] that could be used, which are consistent with the government's future tax system vision as embodied in the MTEF and the IMF Article IV and Standby Program.[61] Other sources of potential financing modalities that are not well articulated in the concept note or policy debate are efficiency gains, specific results-based provider payment, referral system and gatekeeper policies, practice guidelines and treatment protocols, delivery system rationalization to eliminate the inpatient bias, and rationalization of the very comprehensive BBP based on efficiency, affordability, sustainability and catastrophic protection criteria. These areas could be pursued by the task force as they all have important expenditure and/or revenue impacts.

Armenia's health system is unique in both its high level of overall health spending and its extremely heavy reliance on OOP payment. This deprives both the government of needed revenues and the citizens of the financial protection embodied in sharing risks through insurance. Furthermore, it also limits the government's financial leverage over the system. While Armenia's system is designed to help the poor and vulnerable, it needs to transform itself into an efficient and appropriately funded UHI scheme for the entire population. One major financial challenge in this transition is to assure adequate public funding of UHI by transforming much of the 8% of GDP and 8% of household budgets going to OOP and private household health spending, respectively, into additional public resources to support UHI. Having detailed actuarial estimates of the costs of UHI and who will benefit from its implementation provides important information for designing and effectuating this complex funding transition.

---

[60]   Possibly new earmarked or unearmarked taxes (sugary beverages, carbon, financial transactions), voluntary and/or mandatory individual premiums and/or private health insurance options.

[61]   IMF. 2019. Republic of Armenia: 2019 Article IV Consultation. *IMF Country Report*. No. 19/154. Washington, DC.

Actuarial Model Documentation

I. Databases

Data for the actuarial model were curated from the State Health Agency (SHA) database for 2016 Social Package and State Order eligibles. Both programs include different population groups, usually categorized by age, marital status, employment status, disability, and military service. In addition, data for primary health care (PHC) were obtained from the budget, which is based on capitation rates and the assigned population of each facility.

A. Social Package Database

In January 2012, a package of social benefits for public and civil servants was introduced, which included mandatory health insurance. The beneficiaries of the Social Package, irrespective of job position and salary, have access to the Social Package services. The package not only covers health insurance, but it also provides monthly redemption of mortgage credits, tuition fees at accredited universities and vacations in Armenia. This study focused, we focus on the health insurance and the related services covered in the package.

In addition to civil servants, members from the following groups are also included in the Social Package data of 2016

- asylum seekers and their family members;
- beneficiaries included in the poverty beneficiary system with 30.1 and more unit;
- beneficiaries of Social Package;
- compulsory military service personnel (ordinary and lance sergeant);
- disability group – (ii)
- family members of command officials of the Ministry of Defense of Armenia;
- family members of police soldiers; and
- family members of rescue service workers.

Based on discussions with SHA, the Social Package database is supposed to include only the beneficiaries of Social Package, and only due to an error in data entry would someone have any other eligibility group listed. Therefore, cases from other groups were filtered out and all cases in the Social Package came from the database of civil servants.

B.   State Order Database

State Order utilizes public resources to finance, through provider contracts, PHC, and emergency services for all Armenian citizens in the eligibility groups included in the order, with copayment exemptions for the poor and vulnerable. In addition, selected inpatient services are provided for free for the poor, vulnerable, and other specific categories.

The following groups are available in the State Order data (listed in alphabetical order):

- arrested individuals, detainees, and prison inmates;
- asylum seekers and their family members;
- beneficiaries approved by the N44- A Ministerial Order of the Republic of the Armenian Ministry of Health dated 13.01. January 2016;
- beneficiaries included in the poverty (family) beneficiary system with 30.01 and more unit;
- beneficiaries included in the poverty beneficiary (family) system with 36.01 and more unit;
- beneficiaries of Social Package;
- children (up to 18 years of age) under the dispensary control;
- children aged up to 18 years in single parent household;
- children from large families (up to 18 years old) with four and more children;
- children up to age 7 years of age;
- children with disabilities, up to 18 years of age;
- children left without parental care (up to 18 years of age), and individuals considered children left without parental care (aged 18–23 years);
- command officials of the Armenian Ministry of Defense;
- compulsory military service personnel (ordinary and lance sergeant);
- convicted persons;
- disability group – (i);
- disability group – (ii);
- disability group – (iii);
- family members of compulsory military service personnel (ordinary and lance sergeant);
- family members of command officials of the Armenian Ministry of Defense;
- family members of officers registered in the special service personnel reserve of the administrative bodies of the Armenian Ministry of Defense, Armenian police, Armenian national security;
- family members of participants in military actions for the protection of Armenia;
- family members of penitentiary and compulsory service personnel of the Armenian Ministry of Justice;
- family members of the Armenian Police service personnel;
- family members of the rescue service workers;
- former soldiers receiving pensions for long service or disability;
- great Patriotic War veterans and persons equated to them;
- individuals getting care at orphanages and nursing homes;

- individuals holding special civil positions at the administrative bodies of the Armenian Ministry of Defense, police, national security;
- individuals not included in the above-mentioned groups;
- family members of armed forces reservists;
- family members of military service personnel who died while serving in the military or protecting Armenia;
- military and pre-military individuals (inpatient medical care, and the hospital examination for pre-military age population);
- officers registered in the special service personnel reserve of the administrative bodies of the Armenian Ministry of Defense, police, national security;
- participants of the Chernobyl nuclear power plant accident elimination;
- participants in military actions for the protection of Armenia;
- pensioners;
- Armenian police service personnel;
- national security service soldiers;
- recipient of the additional medical examination referred by authorized medical social state body;
- rescue service workers;
- single nonworking pensioners;
- single parent (with child up to 18 years of age);
- soldiers and their family members; and
- women of reproductive age, pregnancy, childbirth, and the postpartum period.

These 45 groups are present in State Order data (2016). Similarly, as with Social Package, we can see an incorrect data entry for beneficiaries of the Social Package. This entry belongs to the Social Package. Upon discussion with SHA, records that were erroneously classified as beneficiaries of the Social Package were affirmed as State Order beneficiaries. These records were distributed to three eligibility groups based on age (pensioners if 63+years of age, State Order–Others if 18–63 years of age, and children aged 0-18 years).

II.   Data Used to Calculate Incidence Rates

A.   Formula for Incidence Rates

The most recent health insurance claims data available at the time of the study were from 2018, but these data had quality issues. Hence, 2016 datasets were used for the actuarial estimates.[62] The base model uses the services as given in State Order and Social Package databases. Furthermore, it assigns the reimbursement rates as decided by the government. For the actuarial estimates, the model requires the number of cases by service name (as defined by the government), the service reimbursement rate

---

[62] In a meeting with SHA and Institute of Health Metrics and Evaluation (IHME), Dr. Mohsen Naghavi from IHME discussed that Armenia's data quality has dropped because the new e-health system does not have professional coders and only requires physicians to input the codes. This increases the likelihood of error in the data. Members of SHA present in the meeting agreed with Dr. Naghavi. Furthermore, he mentioned that IHME has dropped Armenia from 5-star to 3-star for data quality. Therefore, data from 2016 from SHA were used.

(100%), age cohorts, sex, eligibility group, total population in each eligibility group, and incidence rates for each service (utilization) by sex and age eligibility. Data from the United Nations Statistics Division (UNSTAT) were used for the projections. The UN provides data by age-sex for each 5-year interval. Constant absolute change is assumed between intervals, and hence population growth rates for each age-sex cohort are generated based on that. Previously we had 19 different eligibility groups. For ease of modeling, the population was divided into six eligibility groups, including:

- formal sector;
- children;
- pensioners;
- disabled;
- others in State Order; and
- everyone else.

Incidence is calculated as

$$Incidence\ per\ 1000_{bimn} = \frac{Number\ visits_{bimn}}{Total\ enrolled_{bimn}} \times 1000$$

where "b" refers to the government assigned service name, "i" refers to the sex (male or female), "m" is the age cohort (0–9, 10–17, 18–24, 25–44, 45–63, 64–69, 70–74, or >74 years of age), and "n" refers to the eligibility group (children, formal sector, disabled, others in State Order, pensioners, and everyone else).

B.   Calculation by Eligibility Group

1.   Children

Data source. Children are defined solely based on age, unlike the formal sector, which considered the government sector employment and age. All those below 18 are in the children category, regardless of whether we have cases with these age cohorts in the Social Package or State Order. Initially in 2016, only those aged 0–7 years are included in the UHC expenditure, and later all below 18 years of age are included.

Assumptions. For calculating the incidences and fully accounting for all services availed of by the children, data for all those aged 0–17 years of age, from State Order, was appended. Children were divided into three age cohorts: 0–1, 2–7, and 8–17 years of age. Having age cohorts breaking at age 7 allows us to look at the policy change from including 0–7 years to including 0–17 years. The third age cohort, 0–1 years of age has been separated due to the generally higher cost of children in that age group, thus allowing examination of those expenditure estimates.

2.   Formal Sector

Data source. Data from the Social Package are used for formal sector eligibles, and only the services provided in the Social Package are assumed to be covered. All the individuals aged 18–63 years are divided into six cohorts of age-sex: Males/Females (aged 18–24, 25–44, and 45–63 years). Those younger than 18 years and or older than 63 years are excluded from the Social Package database.

Assumptions. Cases are gathered based on the services in the Social Package, and for each service full price (100% reimbursement is applied for calculating the expenditure). None of the services have any copayments in the Social Package, except for costly diagnostic tests. But in this case, full reimbursement rates are used, without considering copayments (that could be accounted for in strategic purchasing and additional variations of the model). Three age cohorts of (18–24, 25–44, and 45–63 years of age) were used because incidences for these groups would differ, and it allows us to look at the expenditures for subgroups rather than one large age cohort of ages 18–63 years. More importantly, a cohort aged 18–24 years could be used as a student group if the government wants.

3.   Pensioners

Data source. Similar to the children eligibility group, pensioners are defined based solely on age. All those older than 63 years are in the pensioners category, regardless of whether we have cases with these age cohorts in the Social Package or State Order. Hence, pensioners are covered by services from both the Social Package and State Order. This group is only based on the age criterion, and therefore it includes even the disabled older than 63 years. The assumption is that only the disabled will have access to disability services, so there is no need to have a separate group for old-age disabled.

Assumptions. For calculating the incidences and fully accounting for all the services availed of by the pensioners, data for all those older than 63 years from the Social Package and State Order, were appended. Pensioners were divided into three age cohorts: 64–69, 70–74, and >74 years of age. Armenia has an aging population, with highest growth in the pensioners cohort. Therefore, dividing it into multiple groups aids in future decision-making related to strategic purchasing. Sixty-three is the retirement age for both men and women in Armenia; hence, those older than 63 fall under the pensioners category.

4.   Others in State Order

Data source. These are individuals from the State Order database who

- are not children aged 0–17 years,
- are not pensioners aged above 63, or
- are not disabled.

Assumptions. These are individuals from the State Order data base who are do not fall into the disability category and are not children or pensioners. They are divided into three age cohorts like the formal sector and disabled: 18–24, 25–44, and 45–63 years of age.

5.   Everyone Else

Data source. This category has no data from the Social Package or State Order, and its members are individuals who cover most of their personal health services through out-of-pocket (OOP) payments. There is no record of them in manual health records or e-health from 2017 onward. Since the hospitals did not have to claim any of these costs from the government, visits were not reported or accounted for. Even after e-health became operational in June 2017, no law was passed to make it mandatory to record OOP visits; hence, data for them is still missing as e-health has no record on OOP payments. Since no data exist, incidence rates for formal sector are used for the everyone else group.

Assumptions. For this cohort, we must rely on assumptions based on both age and population weights. It has three age cohorts: (18–24, 25–44, and 45–63 years of age), the same as the formal sector. We assume that this group has a similar demographic composition as the formal sector; hence, it is reasonable to use the same incidences.

III. Data Used for Population

A. United Nations Statistical Division Data

As mentioned earlier, data from the United Nations Statistical Division (UNSTAT) were used for actuarial projections. UN data provides population breakdowns by age-sex, with 5-year intervals. UNSTAT provides data by the following age cohorts (Table A1.1).

Table A1.1: Formation of Age Cohorts from the United Nations Data

United Nations Age Cohort (years)	In the Actuarial Model (years)	Eligibility Group
0–4	0–1	Children
5–9	2–7	
10–14	8–17	
15–19		
20–24	18–24	Formal Sector, Disabled, Others (State Order), Everyone Else
25–29	25–44	
30–34		
35–39		
40–44		
45–49	45–63	
50–54		
55–59		
60–64		
65–69	64–69	Pensioners
70–74	70–74	
75–79	75+	
80–84		
85–89		
90–94		
95–99		
100+		

Source: United Nations Department of Economic and Social Affairs. World Population Prospects 2019. https://population.un.org/wpp/Download/Standard/Population/.

As seen in Table A1.1, the age cohorts from the UNSTAT categorizations do not correspond directly to the cohorts in the model. Therefore, adjustments were made to the cohorts based on assumptions to calculate the numbers for the relevant cohorts. Table A1.2 shows equations for the cohorts that required adjustments based on assumptions that the population within a cohort is equal for each age.

Table A1.2: Cohorts and Formulas

Cohort 0-1 = [(cohort 0-4)/5]*2

Cohort 2-7 = [(cohort 0-4)/5]*3 + [(cohort 5-9)/5] *3

Cohort 8-17 = [(cohort 5-9)/5]*2 + (cohort 10-14) + [(cohort 15-19)/5] *3

Cohort 18-24 = (cohort 20-24) + [(cohort 15-19)/5] *2

Cohort 45-63 = (cohorts 45-49 + 50-54 + 55-59) + [(cohort 60-64)/5] *4

Cohort 64-69 = (cohorts 65-69) + [(cohort 60-64)/5]

Source: Authors.

B.   Population Adjustments for Formal, Disabled, and Others in State Order

Total Population. Data for the number of people registered in each eligibility group are available from 2018. They were used to generate the same eligibility group populations but based on 2016 population levels. According to UN projections, the population of Armenia in 2016 was approximately 0.7% less than the population in 2018. To generate actuarial estimates, the study used the percentage change in population to adjust the 2018 population eligibility groups to match the 2016 population, which means adult eligibility groups were discounted 0.7% to match the population levels of 2016. Differences are negligible, due to very low population growth rates. The implication of such an assumption is that for each adult subcategory (formal, disability, others in State Order) percentage changes in numbers enrolled between 2016–2018 are the same as the percentage change in total adult population during the same time period. Nevertheless, this might not be the case if from 2016–2018 a policy drastically changes the enrollment numbers in any of these groups, that would deteriorate the reliability of our estimates. Since that has not been the case, and no such major change in enrollment has occurred, it is a reliable assumption to make.

Population by age cohorts. In addition, population breakdown (percentage) in each age cohort in these three groups is assumed to be the same as the overall population breakdown. This is indeed a strong assumption to make. We are assuming that if the 25–44 years age cohort accounts for 37% of the total adult population, then we will have same 37% of total enrolled in each of the three eligibility groups for the same age cohort. Such an assumption implies that enrollment breakdown is same as the total population breakdown, even more importantly it assumes that same assumption applies to each group. For the formal sector and others in the State Order, this assumption should not be an issue as it is fair to assume that enrollments would be same as population breakdowns. In the case of disability groups, it is possible that maybe the 45–63 year age cohort has higher numbers of disabled enrolled than the other two age cohorts, and it could happen only when one age cohort has a significantly higher likelihood of having a disability as compared to other cohorts. Nevertheless, this is not really the case, due to the way disability groups have been defined. All those aged 18–63 years have an almost similar likelihood of being in the disability group. Due to the lack of data, there is no way to know the exact number enrolled for disability in each age cohort.

1.   Children

For the children group, the number of those enrolled in the State Order are calculated using UNSTAT data. Basically, we have information about the total number of enrollees, those numbers are deducted from the total population of Armenia, and the rest is just those who are accessing services using OOP payments. For the children group, the population is equal to the total number of under 18 years of age population in Armenia. For the population within age cohorts, we extrapolated the number of visits by those under 18 years of age.

2.   Pensioners

For pensioners, the same as with children, the calculation was done based on those older than 63 years. Again, there are two approaches to defining the population within age cohorts in pensioners. We used the number of visits from the both packages by age cohorts to assign the same population breakdown for respective age cohorts.

3.   Everyone Else

This eligibility group accounts for Armenians who are not in the system and could fall into any age group (from 18–63 years of age). Population weights within the age cohorts can be assigned based on total population breakdown, or by the number of visits for respective cohorts by using the visits from Social and State Order Packages, assuming that OOP visits will mirror the same distribution as the ones from the Social and State Order. Population projections are presented in Figure A1.1.

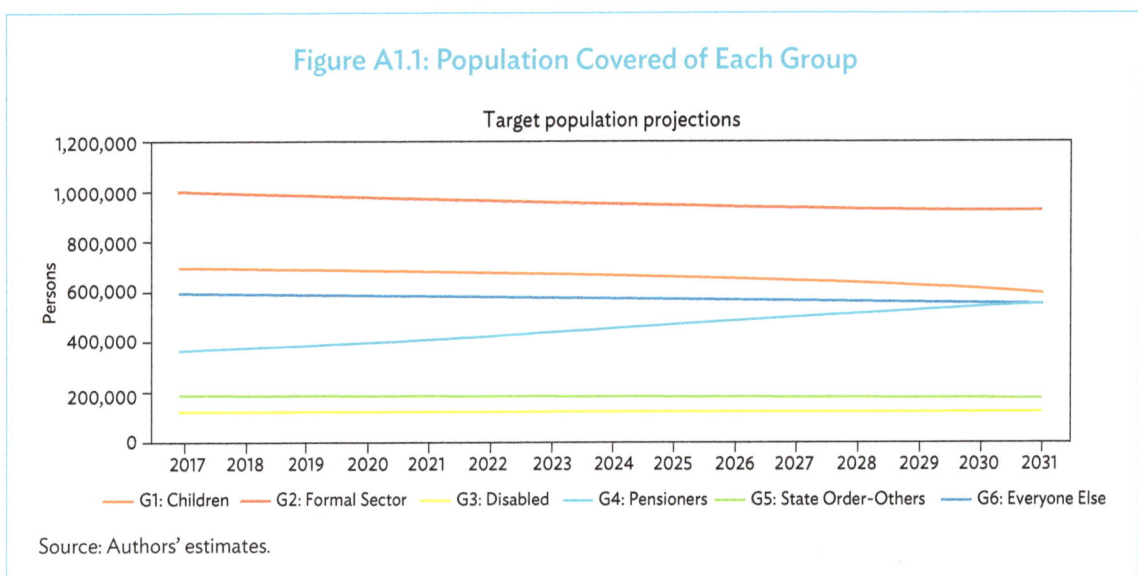

Figure A1.1: Population Covered of Each Group

Source: Authors' estimates.

IV.   Breakdown of Services in the Model

Services can be defined in two broad categories: hospital and PHC. Hospital includes services from Social Package and State Order. PHC includes services offered by outpatient clinics.

A.   Services Covered in Social Package (in alphabetical order)

1.   Abdominal aortic aneurysm surgery, Leriche syndrome (without prosthesis)
2.   Acute surgical / trauma cases diagnostics (medical unfinished) (laboratory and diagnostic studies conducted)
3.   Adeno Tonsillectomy (general anesthesia)
4.   Adenoma Transurethral cutting
5.   Adenoma Transurethral cutting General Practitioner (GP)
6.   Adrenal gland tumor removal
7.   Adrenalectomy adrenal tumor formation or other related (open or endoscopic method)
8.   Amniotic membrane transplantation on stage I
9.   Amniotic membrane transplantation on stage II
10.   Amputation of the arm or thigh region
11.   Amputation of the leg or forearm
12.   Anaerobic Para proctitis excision
13.   Anterior urethral surgery stricture
14.   Appendectomy
15.   Appendectomy (GP)
16.   Appendectomy (Soldier Service [SS] and Social Package [CP])
17.   Appendectomy laparoscopic (GP)
18.   Arm bone, forearm bone, shinbone complex (open fragmentary, intra-articular combined dislocation, soft tissue damage, etc.) fractures
19.   Arm bone, forearm bone, shinbone complex (open fragmentary, intra-articular combined dislocation, soft tissue damage, etc.), fractures (GP)
20.   Arm bone, forearm bone, shinbone fractures simple uncomplicated surgeries
21.   Arm bone, forearm bone, shinbone fractures simple uncomplicated surgeries (GP)
22.   Artery—venous hemodialysis for design fistula
23.   Assisted nephrectomy (hydro nephrosis, bladder, urethra reflux, obstructive mega ureter, kidney stones and other coral stones)
24.   Atypical lung resection
25.   Benign tumors, surgical treatment of diseases salivary stone
26.   Bilateral Vasectomy
27.   Bilateral Vasectomy (GP)
28.   Bladder diseases, bladder reconstructive surgery, which is indicated in different intestinal segments
29.   Bladder diverticulum crossing (without esophageal reflux)
30.   Bladder, ureter and kidney stones crushing and endoscopic removal
31.   Bone grafting bone defect elimination or close by
32.   Bone marrow puncture under local anesthesia (morphological research)

33. Brain and spinal cord cystic tumors, removal echinococcosis
34. Brain or spinal cord residual effects of diseases that need surgical intervention (meningoencephalitis, etc.)
35. Breast biopsy trepan (SS and CP)
36. Breast removal
37. Burn treatment cases
38. Carotid artery surgery
39. Cataract extraction method, including the lens value phacoemulsification
40. Cataract extraction, without the cost of the lens
41. Cervical cryodestruction intravenous anesthetic
42. Chalazion and hysteresis inpatient removal
43. Chest wall reconstruction
44. Choanal atresia, septoplasty (combined)
45. Choanal atresia, septoplasty (combined) (GP)
46. Circular can use rectum resection device (GP)
47. Circular resection for rectal use device can
48. Clavicle, scapula, patella, fibula simple uncomplicated fracture surgery
49. Clavicle, scapula, patella, fibula simple uncomplicated fracture surgery (GP)
50. Clavicle, scapula, patella, fibula, radius, patella, cloves shinbone medial complex (open fragmentary, intra-articular combined dislocation, soft tissue damage, etc.) operations on fractures
51. Clavicle, scapula, patella, fibula, radius, patella, cloves shinbone medial complex (open fragmentary, intra-articular combined dislocation, soft tissue damage, etc.) operations on fractures (GP)
52. Closing double-barreled Stoma
53. Colo proctectomy combined operations
54. Common lesion removal
55. Complete removal of the salivary glands
56. Computed tomography angiography with three parts (including the value of contrast material) (hospital)
57. Computed tomography angiography with three parts (including the value of contrast material) (hospital) (SS, CP)
58. Computed tomography angiography, section 2 (including the value of contrast material) (hospital)
59. Computed tomography angiography, section 2 (including the value of contrast material) (hospital) (SS and CP)
60. Coral kidney stone removal method anatrophic lithotomy
61. Coral kidney stone removal method pyelolithotomy
62. Coronary artery balloon dilatation - using one cylinder
63. Coronary artery balloon dilatation - using two cylinders
64. Coronary geography (including contrast material cost of anesthesia and patient) inpatient treatment (SS and CP)
65. Coronary geography (including the value of contrast material and the patient's anesthesia) (State holding) (CP)
66. Correction of deformities of fingers, arthrosis, arthrodesis, II° complexity musculoligamentous surgeries, bone and soft tissue tumors

67. Correction of deformities of fingers, arthrosis, arthrodesis, I° complexity musculoligamentous surgery, small bone and soft tissue tumors
68. Corrective osteotomy 1 bone fractures not properly connected and not so close to natural and acquired defects and complications of surgical treatment (III° complexity), bone grafting and muscle-tendon
69. Corrective osteotomy 1 bone fractures not properly connected and not so close, natural and acquired defects and complications (III° complexity) surgical treatment of bone and muscle-tendon plastics, bone and soft tissue tumors
70. Corrective osteotomy 1 bone fractures not properly connected and not so close, natural and acquired defects and complications of surgical treatment (I–II° complexity)
71. Corrective osteotomy not properly connected so close and complex reconstructive surgical treatment of fractures, bone and muscle-tendon plastics, Hallux Valgus bone and soft tissue tumors spread III° complexity
72. Corrective osteotomy, nonsurgical treatment of fractures united right, Hallux Valgus I–II° complexity
73. Cross-thigh-hip, thigh-mandibular and peripheral arterial bypass grafting
74. CT angiography is one sector (including the value of contrast material)
75. CT angiography is one sector (including the value of contrast material) (SS and CP)
76. Current joints (shoulder, elbow joint, forearm wrist joint, kneecap-femoral joint, ankle joint) Hip Dysplasia conservative anesthetic treatment
77. Current joints (shoulder, elbow joint, forearm wrist joint, kneecap-femoral joint, ankle joint) Hip Dysplasia surgical correction (plastics, restoration, reconstruction of eardrum)
78. Current metal constructions, shinbone platform, arm bone bones platform (for everyone)
79. Current metal constructions, shinbone platform, arm bone platform (for each) (GP)
80. Current prevalence of infected tissue ablation (GP)
81. Current prevalence of infected tissue removal
82. Dacryocystorhinostomy
83. Dental fractures, secondary
84. Dental fractures, small
85. Diagnostic hysteroscopy
86. Diagnostic laparoscopy (SS and CP)
87. Diagnostic laparotomy (GP)
88. Diagnostic laparotomy (SS and CP)
89. Diagnostic thoracotomy (SS and CP)
90. Diagnostic uterine bleeding or uterine cavity in case of deletion; abortion
91. Diaphragm hernia surgery (SS and CP)
92. Discectomy intervertebral cartilage Hernia
93. Distal pancreatic resection (SS and CP)
94. Double kidney stone lithotripsy
95. Drug eluted 1 stent stenting (SS and CP)
96. Drug eluted 2 stent stenting (in the State)
97. Drug eluted 2 stent stenting (SS and CP)
98. Eardrum, middle and inner ear reconstructive surgery (combined)
99. Eardrum, middle and inner ear reconstructive surgery (not combined)
100. ECG Holter monitoring (SS and CP)
101. Echinococcus liver ablation (GP)
102. Echinococcus liver ablation (SS and CP)

103. Electro cardioversion (SS and CP)
104. Endometria centers coagulation or endometrium cyst removal, retro cervical endometriosis, salpingostomy
105. Endoscopic bladder neck cut
106. Endovascular treatment of cerebral vascular diseases used in more than one value for each additional micro catheter
107. Endovascular treatment of cerebral vascular diseases used in more than one value for each additional Mirage 0,008 micro catheter
108. Endovascular treatment of the brain (including one micro catheter, onyx cost per micro spiral or disease)
109. Events requiring resuscitation and intensive therapy of diseases and conditions included in the list of diseases and conditions of medical treatment Level I intensive services organizations
110. Events requiring resuscitation and intensive therapy of diseases and conditions included in the list of diseases and conditions of medical treatment level II intensive services organizations
111. Events requiring resuscitation and intensive therapy of diseases and conditions included in the list of diseases and conditions treatment level III intensive care services with medical organizations
112. Excision margin bowel fistula
113. External hemorrhoids nodes radiofrequency ablation method
114. External urethral opening cyst removal
115. External urethral opening cyst removal (GP)
116. Extirpation rectum
117. Eye anterior segment reconstruction
118. Eyeball removal transplantation, transplantation evisceration
119. Face or neck soft tissue tumors / D => 3 cm / removal
120. Fist finger plaster immobilization (SS and CP)
121. Fixation spinal surgeries, primary or background spondylodesis different constructions (with no value system)
122. Focal surgery for intestinal pathologies (SS and CP)
123. Foot fingers plaster immobilization
124. Gallbladder removal (GP)
125. Gallbladder removal (SS and CP)
126. Gastrectomy (GP)
127. Gastrectomy (SS and CP)
128. Great combinations and tendon damage surgeries
129. Great fat disposal (SS and CP)
130. Great fat removal (GP)
131. Hand, foot (except talus and calcaneus) 3 and more bone complex (open fragmentary, intra-articular combined dislocation, soft tissue damage, etc.) operations on fractures
132. Hand, foot bones simple uncomplicated fracture surgery 2
133. Hand, foot one simple uncomplicated fractures, bone surgery
134. Hand, foot one simple uncomplicated fractures, bone surgery (GP)
135. Hemodialysis conducted in acute renal failure (1 session)
136. Hemorrhoidectomy
137. Hemorrhoidectomy (GP)

138. Herniotomy (without a net value) (GP)
139. Herniotomy (without a net value) (SS and CP)
140. Herniotomy (without the net cost)
141. Herniotomy laparoscopic (without a net value) (GP)
142. Highmoritis and/ or ethmoidectomy (general anesthesia)
143. Highmoritis and/ or ethmoidectomy (general anesthesia) (GP)
144. Hip and pelvic bone complex (open fragmentary, intra-articular combined dislocation, soft tissue damage, etc.) operations on fractures
145. Hip and pelvic bone fractures simple uncomplicated surgeries
146. Hip and pelvic bone fractures simple uncomplicated surgeries (GP)
147. Hip knee, shoulder, ankle joint diagnostic arthroscopy (for each study)
148. Hip, knee, shoulder and ankle joint diagnostic arthroscopy
149. Hip, knee, shoulder and ankle joint therapeutic arthroscopy I° complexity (joint debridement partial synovectomies, removal of meniscus articular, chondromatosis bodies, folds and other pathological changes correction)
150. Hip, knee, shoulder and ankle joints therapeutic arthroscopy III° complexity (combined intra-articular and extra articular reconstructive operations)
151. Hip, knee, shoulder and ankle joints therapeutic arthroscopy II° complexity (intra-articular bone-cartilage surgery and rehabilitation, subtotal synovectomy damaged and contaminated system intra-articular ligament reconstruction)
152. Hydro nephrosis (plastic)
153. Hysteroscopy laparoscopy under control
154. II level intensive care / high /
155. Ileo-Colostomy design (GP)
156. Ileo-shapes Colostomy
157. In case of gastric cancer surgery pathologies (SS and CP)
158. Internal hemorrhoids ligation junctions
159. Internal hemorrhoids ligation of nodes (GP)
160. Intra-orbital tumor removal
161. IV complexity of reconstructive surgical treatment
162. IV complexity of reconstructive surgical treatment (large bone fractures not united)
163. Jaws and facial reconstructive surgery for functional
164. Keratoplasty
165. Kidney abscess drainage and cutting
166. Kidney stone lithotripsy through (up to 4,000 stroke)
167. Kidney, transurethral and intra-bladder cysts crossing
168. Laparoscopic cholecystectomies (GP)
169. Laparoscopic cholecystectomies (SS and CP)
170. Laparoscopic Gallbladder Removal
171. Laparoscopic sterilization of pulp; ovarian cauterization, salpingolysis, fibroblastic, LUNA; Chromoendoscopy, laparoscopy, terrace wall plastics, conservative myomectomy
172. Large joints (knee-joint and hip joint) dislocation conservative treatment
173. Large joints (knee-joint and hip joint) dislocation conservative treatment (GP)
174. Large joints (knee-joint and hip joint) dislocation surgical correction (plastics, restoration, reconstruction of eardrum)
175. Large joints (p / a, knee-joint, s / he joint, shoulder, elbow joint) total endoprosthesis / reconstruction of eardrum without endoprosthesis value

176. Large joints (p / a, knee-joint, s / he joint, shoulder, elbow joint) total endoprosthesis / no reconstruction without endoprosthesis value /
177. Large metal structures, platform thigh, arm nail, nail shin, thigh nail (for everyone)
178. Large metal structures, platform thigh, arm nail, nail shin, thigh nail (for each) (GP)
179. Lens vitrectomy
180. Ligament damage and great combinations of complicated surgeries
181. Lobectomy
182. Lung decortication
183. Lymph node biopsy: histological study of open pit (SS and CP)
184. Magistral and balloon dilatation of peripheral arteries using a balloon
185. Magistral and peripheral arterial stenting and balloon dilatation for additional use during each cylinder
186. Magistral and peripheral arterial stenting one stent
187. Magistral and peripheral artery stenting, 2-stent
188. Magistral and peripheral artery stenting, the stent
189. Magnetic resonance imaging (contrast material without cost) (hospital)
190. Magnetic resonance imaging (contrast material without cost) (hospital) (SS and CP)
191. Magnetic resonance imaging (including the value of contrast material) (hospital)
192. Major vascular surgery, thoracic and lumbar sympathectomy, Linton surgery
193. Many kidney stone removal (three or more stones) surgery
194. Meatostenosis (myotomy)
195. Medial or lateral neck cyst excision (general anesthesia)
196. Metal construction of large, foreign body removal
197. Metal construction of large, foreign body removal of (GP)
198. Minor damage tendons and combinations of complicated surgeries
199. Minor damage tendons and combinations of complicated surgeries (GP)
200. Minor damage tendons and combinations of operations
201. Minor damage tendons and combinations of operations (GP)
202. Nasal and sinus cavities and related operations, septoplasty (not combined)
203. Nasal and sinus cavities and related operations, septoplasty (not combined) (GP)
204. Nasal and sinus polyps (general anesthesia)
205. Nasal and sinus polyps (general anesthesia) (GP)
206. Nasal fractures reposition (general anesthesia) (GP)
207. Nasal respiration recovery operations
208. Nasal respiration recovery operations (GP)
209. Needles and screws (one unit per section)
210. Neoplasms intra-cavity radiation treatment (1 session price), not older than 10 session
211. Neurolysis neurorrhaphy
212. Neurosurgical minor surgeries
213. Non- drug eluted stenting with one stent
214. Nose, face, neck, ear reconstructive surgery (combined)
215. Nose, face, neck, ear reconstructive surgery (not combined)
216. Obstruction without necrosis (GP)
217. One Drug eluted stent one non-medical eluted stent (SS and CP)
218. One Drug eluted stent two non-medical eluted stent
219. Open adenectomy
220. Operations associated with the nasal septum Deviation (general anesthesia) (GP)

221. Operations at TOT- who incontinence (without the cost of ribbon)
222. Operations obstruction case (GP)
223. Operations of chronic hypertrophic rhinitis (general anesthesia) (GP)
224. Operations of chronic hypertrophic rhinitis (local anesthesia)
225. Operations of ulcerative disease (GP)
226. Operations on choledochus (GP)
227. Operations on choledochus (SS and CP)
228. Operations on chronic hypertonic rhinitis (general anesthetic)
229. Operations on the breast (sectoral resection, cyst removal, etc.)
230. Operations related to the nasal septum Deviation (general anesthesia)
231. Orchiectomy
232. Orchiectomy (GP)
233. Orchiectomy bilateral
234. Osteomyelitis complicated case pelvis, long bones sequester- and neurectomy
235. Pan hysterectomy ileo- paraaortic lymph dissection, widened vulvectomy groin-ileocolic lymph dissection
236. Pan retinal photocoagulation (one eye)
237. Papilla overgrowth removal
238. Para proctitis coccyx epithelial fistula incision (GP)
239. Para proctitis excision bowel lumen
240. Para renal cysts crossing
241. Para Tonsillitis abscesses crossing (general anesthesia)
242. Paraproctitis Excision bowel lumen (GP)
243. Paronychia, ingrown nail, nail removal
244. Paronychia, ingrown nail, nail removal (GP)
245. Partition operations on
246. Patients with primary research hospital for diagnosis specification (infectious diseases, oncology and hematology services)
247. Patients with primary research hospital for diagnosis specification (infectious diseases, oncology and hematology services) (SS and CP)
248. Patients with primary research hospital for diagnosis specification (infectious diseases, oncology and hematology services) (GP)
249. Percutaneous cystostomy
250. Percutaneous nephrostomy
251. Perianal condyloma removal (GP)
252. Periphery surgery on the arteries, peripheral endarterectomy (GP)
253. Periphery surgery on the arteries, peripheral endarterectomy
254. Phalanges fingers, meta carpal bone and tarsus bone fistula removal debridement, sequester- and neurectomy
255. Pharynx tumor removal mouth (general anesthesia)
256. Phlegmonous and abscess and maxillofacial region (general anesthesia)
257. Phlegmonous, Abscesses opening (GP)
258. Phlegmonous, Abscesses opens
259. Pins and screws for one segment (per unit) (GP)
260. Plaster immobilization of fractures (lower limb) (GP)
261. Plaster immobilization of fractures (lower limb) (SS and CP)
262. Plaster immobilization of fractures (upper extremity) (GP)

263. Plaster immobilization of fractures (upper extremity) (SS and CP)
264. Plastics of Phimosis
265. Plastics of Phimosis (GP)
266. Pneumonectomy
267. Polypectomy through colonoscopy
268. Polypectomy through colonoscopy (GP)
269. Polytrauma combined operations (Vascular Surgery)
270. Posterior abdominal organ or tumor removal
271. Posterior urethral surgery stricture
272. Posterior urethral valve endoscopic cutting
273. Primary research hospital patients diagnose conditions to verify the Day Hospital (infectious diseases, oncology and hematology services)
274. Promontory fixation (uterus, vagina and terrace walls of muscle control)
275. Radical assisted nephrectomy for tumors of
276. Radical cystectomy without rehabilitation intervention ureterocutaneostomy
277. Radical prostatectomy
278. Radius, patella, shinbone fractures medial cloves simple uncomplicated surgeries
279. Radius, patella, shinbone fractures medial cloves simple uncomplicated surgeries (GP)
280. Reconstructive surgery for colon
281. Reconstructive surgery of the large intestine (without head Value)
282. Rectal resection with stoma
283. Rectocele Troubleshooting
284. Removal common lesion (GP)
285. Removal of affected tissue (GP)
286. Removal of benign neoplasms of the perineum and vaginal walls, uterine neck amputation; Removal of cricoid, electro conization of the uterus neck; resectoscope hysteroscopy
287. Removal of epithelial coccygeal fistula
288. Removal of epithelial coccygeal fistula (GP)
289. Removal of liver echinococcosis
290. Removal of lung echinococcosis
291. Removal of lymph nodes in the neck-sided
292. Removal of perianal condyloma
293. Removal of pointed condylomas
294. Removal of small metallic parts
295. Removal of small tumors (general anesthesia) (GP)
296. Removal of small tumors (general anesthesia) (SS and CP)
297. Removal of small tumors (local anesthesia) (GP)
298. Removal of small tumors (local anesthesia) (SS and CP)
299. Removal of the brain and skull base tumors deep parts
300. Removal of the spine and spinal cord tumors
301. Removal of the spleen (GP)
302. Removal of tumors of the chest wall thoracic minor surgeries without general anesthesia
303. Renal biopsy (SS and CP)
304. Resection of colon (without head Value) reconnection
305. Resection of colon (without head Value) reconnection (GP)
306. Resection of colon with stoma
307. Resuscitation I level / big

308. Retinal pneumatic retinopexy and detachment laser coagulation
309. Scar phimosis (circumcision)
310. Short curb (cutting)
311. Short-term hospitalization / great narrow specialty
312. Short-term or small-scale or small expenditure day inpatient hospital care setting (GP) (capacities and CP)
313. Short-term or small-scale or small expenditure day inpatient hospital care of (specialized) (SS and CP)
314. Short-term or small-scale or small expenditure hospital care
315. Short-term or small-scale or small expenditure hospital care (GP)
316. Short-term or small-scale or small expenditure hospital care (specialized) (SS and CP)
317. Silicone oil removal
318. Sinus trabeculectomy non-invasive form of surgery, removal of stitches
319. Sinus trabeculectomy surgery (traditional method)
320. Sinus trabeculectomy, cataract extraction
321. Small joints of the wrist and ankle dislocation conservative treatment communicative or general anesthesia (outpatient) (SS and CP)
322. Small metal construction of the removal of (GP)
323. Small metal constructions, cloves platform, platform forearm, collarbone platform (for everyone)
324. Small vascular surgery
325. Small wounds bandage without stitches
326. Spermatic cyst removal
327. Spermatic veins, high crosses
328. Spermatic veins, high crosses (GP)
329. Spermatic veins, inguinal microscopic method
330. Stenting with one non-drug eluted stent (SS and CP)
331. Stenting with drug eluted 3 stents
332. Stenting with drug eluted 4 stents
333. Stereotomy average volume (GP)
334. Stereotomy radical lymph dissection volume (GP)
335. Stereotomy small volume (GP)
336. Stereotomy volume (GP)
337. Strabismus correction muscle transplantation
338. Strumectomy average volume
339. Strumectomy radical lymph dissection volume
340. Strumectomy volume
341. Sub-articular fracture (outpatient) (SS and CP)
342. Subacute or chronic hematoma of surgery
343. Subtotal abdominal hysterectomy salpingectomia, ovariectomy, adnexectomy (in case of inflammatory tumors), ovarian cyst and / or removal cystoma
344. Talus and calcaneus complex (open fragmentary, intra-articular combined dislocation, soft tissue damage, etc.) operations on fractures
345. Tapes removal
346. Tapes removal of (GP)
347. Terminal Serious Glaucoma Alcoholization
348. Testicular membranes hydrocele surgery

349. Testicular membranes hydrocele surgery (GP)
350. The citizen computer X-ray tomography is more than one place
351. The primary surgical treatment of injuries caused by animals
352. Therapeutic intra-articular puncture
353. Therapeutic profile (including infection) conservative treatment and surgical wards, day hospitals, without any accompanying diseases and complications
354. Therapeutic profile (including infections) and accompanying surgical wards conservative treatment (requiring separate treatment) diseases and / or complications of diseases
355. Therapeutic profile (including infections) and accompanying surgical wards conservative treatment (requiring separate treatment) diseases and / or complications of the disease (GP)
356. Therapeutic profile (including infections) and accompanying surgical wards conservative treatment (requiring separate treatment) diseases and / or complications of diseases of the Day Hospital
357. Therapeutic profile (including infections) and accompanying surgical wards conservative treatment (in case of requiring separate treatment) of diseases and / or complications of diseases Day Hospital (GP)
358. Therapeutic profile (including infections) and surgical wards conservative treatment without concomitant diseases and complications
359. Therapeutic profile (including infections) and surgical wards conservative treatment without any accompanying diseases and complications (GP)
360. Therapeutic profile (including infections) and surgical wards conservative treatment without concomitant diseases and complications in the Day Hospital (GP)
361. Thigh, arm bone, shinbone fistula removal debridement
362. Thigh, arm bone, shinbone sequester- and neurectomy
363. Thoracic surgery lymphadenectomy
364. Thoracic surgery, lymph biopsy
365. Thoracoscopy (SS and CP)
366. Throat resection laryngoscopy design
367. Throat Tumor Ablation (general anesthesia)
368. Throat Tumor Ablation (local anesthesia)
369. Tonsillectomy (general anesthesia)
370. Tonsillectomy (general anesthesia) (GP)
371. Tonsillectomy (local anesthesia)
372. Tonsillectomy (local anesthesia) (GP)
373. TOT- total Abdominal hysterectomy, the vaginal hysterectomy laparoscopic assistance (LAVH) TOT- who, vaginal hysterectomy Triplex TOT- who, in surgery pro hysterectomy prolapses who TOT-
374. Total Abdominal hysterectomy tumor spread to the adjacent organs
375. Total abdominal hysterectomy, vaginal hysterectomy Triplex, surgery post hysterectomy prolapses case
376. Total laparoscopic hysterectomy; colpohysterectomy; RECTOR-vaginal area abdominal laparoscopic removal vulvectomy
377. Tracheostomy
378. Trans anal rectal foreign body removal
379. Trans anal tumor removal
380. Trans rectal prostate biopsy, histological examination

381. Transurethral resection of bladder tumors
382. Trepan biopsy local anesthesia (histological examination)
383. Tumor radiation treatment (1 session price), not older than 35 session
384. Tumor removal mouth pharynx (local anesthesia)
385. Tympanoplasty (general anesthesia)
386. Ureter or kidney stone removal relapse double surgery
387. Ureter stenting
388. Ureter stone removal surgery
389. Urethral diverticulum excision
390. Urethrocystoscopy diagnostic purposes (SS and CP)
391. Uvulopalatopharyngoplasty, tonsillectomy, tongue root ultrasound
392. Vaginal hysterectomy; surgery in Manchester
393. Vaginal septum cutting, Bartholin gland cyst removal, abscess capsule removal opening
394. Vascular surgery CAVA filter installation (SS and CP)
395. Venectomy, condition precludes thrombectomy (Thrombectomy)
396. Venectomy, condition precludes thrombectomy (trombembolectomy) (GP)
397. Ventral hernia great (without a net value) (GP)
398. Ventral hernia great (without a net value) (SS and CP)
399. Vesicle internal drainage or removal of the pancreas (SS and CP)
400. Vitrectomy
401. Wound primary surgical treatment, and tailoring
402. Wound primary surgical treatment, and tailoring (GP)
403. Wrist and ankle dislocation of small joints, surgical correction (GP)
404. Wrist, heel bone, fibula fistula removal debridement
405. Wrist, metacarpal bone, heel, tarsus and interdigital articular general anesthetic Amputation
406. X-ray computer tomography (brain, orbitalis pituitary, Dental, neck, chest, breast, abdomen, pelvis, spine, according to segments of the cervical, thoracic, low back, upper and lower limbs) course. place. (hospital)
407. ТУР bladder biopsy (SS and CP)

B. Services Covered in State Order (in alphabetical order)

1. Abdominal aortic aneurysm surgery via endovascular method (without the cost of prosthesis)
2. Abdominal-reconstructive /adult
3. Acute myocardial infarction, including intensive therapy/ without reanimation services
4. Acute myocardial infarction, including Level I reanimation services
5. Acute myocardial infarction, including Level II reanimation services
6. Acute myocardial infarction, including Level III reanimation services
7. Acute poisoning /adult
8. Acute urinary retention /adult
9. Additional each cylinder used during magistral and peripheral arterial stenting and balloon dilatation
10. Additional each cylinder used during magistral and peripheral arterial stenting and balloon dilatation (state participation)
11. Additional passage ablation

12. Aid at rural health centers
13. Allergological /adult
14. Allergological day care /adult
15. Average metal constructions, shinbone platform, arm bone bones platform (GP)
16. Benign tumor surgery
17. Benign tumors surgery /adult
18. Bladder, ureter and kidney stones crushing and endoscopic removal
19. Bone fractures, dislocation, plaster Installation / nonsurgical/ general, large
20. Bone fractures, dislocation, plaster installation /nonsurgical / large
21. Bronchitis, pneumonia
22. Cardiac surgery / adult (state participation)
23. Cardiological /adult
24. Cardiological, day care /adult
25. Chemical treatment of the blood (except for acute leukemia), malignant diseases (without chemotherapy medications) /adult
26. Chemical treatment of the blood (except for acute leukemia), malignant diseases (without chemotherapy medications) /day care/ adult
27. Chemotherapy of the malignant neoplasm (without costs of the chemotherapy medications) / day care / adult
28. Chemotherapy of the malignant neoplasm (without costs of the chemotherapy medications)/adult
29. Chemotherapy of the malignant neoplasm (without costs of the chemotherapy medications)
30. Chemotherapy treatment of the Acute leukemia (without cost of the chemotherapy medications) / adult, day care
31. Chemotherapy treatment of the Acute leukemia (without cost of the chemotherapy medications) /adult
32. Chemotherapy treatment of the Acute leukemia (without cost of the chemotherapy medications) /day care
33. Communicable (infectious) / adult
34. Complex treatment of malignant neoplasm /adult
35. Complicated deliveries `III degree of complexity
36. Coronary angiography (including expenses of the contrast material and anesthesia of the patient) during hospital care (SS and SP)
37. Coronary angiography during hospital care
38. Coronary angiography during hospital care
39. Coronary angiography only examination
40. Coronary artery dilatation with one-balloon cylinder / adult
41. Coronary artery dilatation with two-balloon cylinder / adult
42. Delivery with caesarean section II degree of complexity
43. Diagnostic angiography of the brain (including the value of contrast material and anesthesia of the patient) during hospital treatment
44. Diagnostic angiography of the brain (including the value of contrast material and anesthesia of the patient), only examination
45. Double lithotripsy
46. Endocrinological /adult
47. Endocrinological day care / adult

48. Endovascular reconstructive surgery /adult (with state participation)
49. Examination based on medical and Social Expertise Committees referral at the day care hospital /adult
50. Examination based on medical and Social Expertise Committees referral at the day care hospital /adult
51. Examination based on medical and Social Expertise Committees referral /adult
52. Examination based on the referral of the forensic medical expert /adult
53. Examination based on the referral of the forensic medical expert at the day care /adult
54. Extra cylinder used during coronary artery stenting and balloon dilatation
55. Fistulation, reconstruction and closure of blood vessels patients receiving hemodialysis, large
56. Gastroenterological /adult
57. Gastroenterological day care /adult
58. General gynecological /adult
59. General pediatrics
60. General Pediatrics day care
61. General Surgical
62. General Surgical /adult
63. General Surgical /adult/1.08
64. General therapeutic
65. General therapeutic /1.08
66. General therapeutic day care
67. General therapeutic day care /1.08
68. Gynecological (Conserve) day care / adult
69. Gynecological /adult
70. Hypertonic crisis / adult
71. Implementation and reimplementation of the cardiac pacemakers duplex devices / for 8–10 year
72. Kidney colic/adult
73. Kidney stone lithotripsy through (up to 4,000 stroke)
74. Large metal structures, platform thigh, arm nail, nail shin, thigh nail (for everyone)
75. Magistral and balloon dilatation of peripheral arteries using one balloon
76. Magistral and peripheral artery stenting (state participation)
77. Magistral and peripheral artery stenting with three stent (state participation)
78. Magistral and peripheral artery stenting with two stent (state participation)
79. Magnetic resonance imaging (including the cost of the contrast material) (hospital)
80. Magnetic resonance imaging (without cost of the contrast material) (outpatient)
81. Magnetic resonance imaging (without the cost of the contrast material) (hospital)
82. Maxillofacial /adult
83. Microsurgical / adult
84. Minor surgical interventions / adult
85. Needles and screws for one deployment (one unit)
86. Nephrological /adult
87. Nephrological /adult/ Day care
88. Neurological / adult / Day Care
89. Neurological /adult
90. Neurosurgical / adult

91. Neurosurgical / large / nonsurgical intervention
92. Nonsurgical treatment of the bone fractures, the duration of the treatment of 15 days or more / adult
93. Nonsurgical treatment of the bone fractures, the duration of the treatment of 15 days or more /general/ adult
94. Nonsurgical treatment of the bone fractures, up to 15 days or more / adult
95. Nonsurgical treatment of the bone fractures, up to 15 days or more /general/ adult
96. One-month care of the kidney transplant patient /adult
97. One-month care of the kidney transplant patient /child
98. Operations of external genital organs and vaginal wall injury / adult
99. Ophthalmologic at hospital /adult
100. Ophthalmological, day care /adult
101. Ophthalmology with small surgical intervention / adult
102. Ophthalmology with small surgical intervention/general, adult
103. Orthopedic
104. Orthopedic / adult
105. Orthopedic day care /adult
106. Orthopedic, surgical intervention
107. Orthopedic, surgical intervention /adult
108. Otolaryngologic
109. Otolaryngologic /adult
110. Otolaryngologic day acre / adult
111. Over one deployment of computerized X-ray tomography for the same patient (hospital)
112. Partial refund of the kidney transplantation /adult
113. Pathologic anatomy / 1-autopsy/ adult
114. Pathology of pregnancy
115. Pathology of pregnancy / Transfer case
116. Percutaneous nephrostomy
117. Peripheral vascular, renal artery stenting without stent expenses
118. Plastic-Reconstructive / adult
119. Premature and newborn
120. Pre-military expertise at the Hospital
121. Pre-military expertise during shock syndrome, Familial Mediterranean fever Hospital and Bedwetting
122. Proctological /adult
123. Psychosomatic / adult
124. Pulmonological /adult
125. Pulmonology day care/ adult
126. Pustular surgery (including blood sowing established sepsis) / adult
127. Radiation injuries /adult
128. Radiation injuries at day care /adult
129. Radiation treatment of the malignant neoplasm / day care
130. Radiation treatment of the malignant neoplasm / day care / adult
131. Radiation treatment of the malignant neoplasm /adult
132. Radiation treatment of the malignant neoplasm, radiological department (adult)
133. Radiation treatment of the malignant neoplasm, radiological department (adult) (day care)
134. Reanimation and intensive care of the infants and children up to 1

135. Reanimation I level / adult
136. Reanimation II level / adult
137. Reanimation III level / adult
138. Rehabilitation at the hospital
139. Rehabilitation center (caretaker)
140. Rehabilitation Day Care
141. Rehabilitation Day Care, /adult
142. Rehabilitation treatment /adult
143. Rehabilitation treatment at child health resorts
144. Rehabilitation treatment at Germuk Sanatorium/adult
145. Rehabilitation treatment at Vanadzor Sanatorium
146. Rehabilitation treatment Gandzaghbyur Sanatorium
147. Rehabilitation urology / adult
148. Removal of the many kidney stones (three or more stones)
149. Rheumatological /adult
150. Rheumatological day care/ adult
151. Short-term hospitalization / adult narrow specialty
152. Short-term hospitalization / general / adult
153. Short-term hospitalization / narrow specialty / adult / day
154. Short-term hospitalization /adult
155. Short-term hospitalization /general / adults / day care
156. Small metal constructions, cloves platform, platform forearm, collarbone platform (for everyone)
157. Speleotherapy
158. Speleotherapy /adult
159. Stenting with four drug eluted stent / adult
160. Stenting with one drug eluted stent (state participation)
161. Stenting with one drug eluted stent / adult
162. Stenting with one drug eluted stent and one non-drug eluted stent (state participation)
163. Stenting with one non-drug eluted stent / adult
164. Stenting with three drug eluted stent
165. Stenting with three drug eluted stent (state participation)
166. Stenting with two drug eluted stent (state participation)
167. Stenting with two drug eluted stent / adult
168. Stenting with two drug eluted stent and two non-drug eluted stent / adult
169. Stenting with two non-drug eluted stent (state participation)
170. Stroke including the Level I reanimation services
171. Stroke including the Level II reanimation services
172. Stroke including the Level III reanimation services
173. Stroke, including intensive therapy /without reanimation services
174. Surgical treatment of bone fractures / adult
175. Surgical treatment of bone fractures / general, adult
176. Surgical treatment of malignant neoplasm
177. Surgical treatment of malignant neoplasm /adult
178. Symptomatic treatment of blood diseases /adult
179. Symptomatic treatment of malignant neoplasm / day care / adult
180. Symptomatic treatment of malignant neoplasm /adult/

181. Therapeutic profile (including infections) and conservative treatment of the accompanying (requiring separate treatment) diseases and /or diseases with complications at surgical departments
182. Thoracic surgery / adult
183. Tonsillectomy, adenoidectomy General anesthesia
184. Tonsillectomy, adenoidectomy general anesthesia / adult
185. Tonsillectomy, adenoidectomy local anesthesia / adult
186. Tonsillectomy, adenoidectomy local anesthetic
187. Treatment of the acute attack of glaucoma without surgical intervention /adult
188. Treatment of the other blood diseases /adult
189. Treatment of the spinal patients at hospital /adult
190. Ureter stenting
191. Urological
192. Urological /adult
193. Urological day care / adult
194. Uterine cavity deletion at hospital /adult
195. Vascular surgery / adult
196. Vascular surgery with CAVA filter installation (SS and SP)
197. Vascular surgery with CAVA filter installation / adult
198. Vascular surgery with nonsurgical intervention / adult
199. Vitreoretinal surgery (at ophthalmological hospital) /Adult
200. X -ray computer tomography (brain, orbitalis pituitary, dental, neck, chest, breast, abdomen, pelvis, spine, according to segments of the cervical, thoracic, low back, upper and lower limbs) course. place hospital

Services are defined differently in both programs. The Social Package has 407 services, and State Order has 200 services. We cannot clearly assume here that either one provides more services than the other. Services covered are different, and similarly the prices are also different. Social Package reimbursement rates are higher than State Order. Social Package defines services more narrowly, while State Order defines them more broadly; this is also one of the reasons that State Order has fewer services. For example, in Social Package, there are two x-ray services but in State Order there is only one.

There is no clear mapping between Social Package and State Order services, hence, there is no way to know which services are essentially the same. For this study, services from both packages have been used, which provides us a more detailed model as incidences are calculated for each service in each package.

Both services are included in the model separately, without using any mapping, but to match the prices, prices of State Order services were increased by a factor of ~2.3 to match the prices of Social Package. This factor was derived by adding the prices of all Social Package services and dividing by its number of services, giving us an average price, and then the same was done for State Order services. Then the average price of Social Package services was divided by the average price of State Order services, which gave us this factor.

Also, none of the services have copayments, except for costly diagnostic tests, which mainly include magnetic resonance imaging. In that case, for the base model, and for accurate total expenditure projections based on actuarial estimates, total price has been used instead of deducting any copayments. Therefore, the model assumes that there are no copayments.

C. Calculation of Price Factor

Using Stata software,[63] Social Package and State Order claims data reimbursement values were collapsed and then divided by the number of observations for each file, providing us with the average reimbursement per visit for each claims data file (Social Package and State Order). Then the Social Package average reimbursement per visit was divided by the State Order average reimbursement per visit, and that gave us the factor of ~2.3 that was used to increase the State Order prices to match the Social Package prices.

1. Average reimbursement per visit for State Order: AMD114,785
2. Average reimbursement per visit for Social Package: AMD259,997
3. Factor = 259997/114785 = 2.265

V. Summary of Eligibility Groups, Data Sources for Incidences, and Services in the Actuarial Model

Table A1.3: Eligibility Groups–Data Sources–Age Cohorts

Eligibility Group	Program Expanded and Data Source for Incidences	Age Cohorts (years)
Children	State Order	0–1, 2–7, 8–17
Formal sector	Social Package	18–24, 25–44, 45–63
Disabled	State Order	18–24, 25–44, 45–63
Pensioners	State Order (if unemployed)	64–69, 70–74, 75–
	Social Package (if employed)	
Others in State Order	State Order	18–24, 25–44, 45–63
Everyone Else	Social Package	18–24, 25–44, 45–63

Source: Authors.

[63] The following Stata codes were used:

```
**following Stata code was run on each claims data file to calculate the average reimbursement per visit**
**after opening the file**
destring Reimbusement,replace
gen dummy=1
collapse (sum) Reimbursement dummy
gen average_social = Reimbursement / dummy
**using the data viewer, we will have the average reimbursements per visit**
```

VI.   Descriptive Statistics and Expenditure Estimates

A.   Population Numbers for Each Eligibility Group for Expansion

Table A1.4 shows the population covered and their assumptions:

Table A1.4: Population Covered and Assumptions

Eligibility Group	Covered Population (No.)	Age Cohorts (years)	Program Expanded	Assumption (Group-Specific)
Children	697,528	• 0–1 • 2–7 • 8–17	• State Order • Outpatient Drugs (ILCS)	• All aged <18 years • Population from UNSTAT (No.)
Formal Sector	720,753	• 18–24 • 25–44 • 45–63	• Social Package • State Order (military) • Outpatient Drugs (ILCS)	• 53% of workers aged 18–63 years • Formal sector from ARMSTAT (%) • Military continues to have State Order
Disabled	131,674	• 18–24 • 25–44 • 45–63	• State Order • Outpatient Drugs (ILCS)	• Aged 18–63 years • Numbers from Ministry of Labor and Social Affairs • Aggregated disabled groups I, II, III
Pensioners	364,266	• 64–69 • 70–74 • 75+	• State Order (if unemployed) • Social Package (if employed) • Outpatient Drugs (ILCS)	• All aged >63 (years) • Population from UNSTAT (No.)
Others— State Order	188,312	• 18–24 • 25–44 • 45–63	• State Order • Outpatient Drugs (ILCS)	• Those in State Order but not included in any of the other three groups • 18–63 • State Order participants aged 18–63 years and not disabled (No.)
Everyone Else	895,441	• 18–24 • 25–44 • 45–63	• Social Package • Outpatient Drugs (ILCS)	• Left from total population • Deducting all the above numbers from total population

ILCS = Integrated Living Conditions Survey, UNSTAT = United Nations Statistics Division.
United Nations Department of Economic and Social Affairs. *World Population Prospects 2019*. https://population.un.org/wpp/Download/Standard/Population/; World Bank. 2017. *Integrated Living Conditions Survey 2017*. https://microdata.worldbank.org/index.php/catalog/3591.

B.   Outpatient Drugs Calculation

Outpatient drugs expenditure was estimated from the ILCS 2016 dataset. ILCS data include questions relevant to outpatient drugs expenditure for everyone in the survey. It also provides their age, gender, employment status, and social category. Outpatient expenditure is provided for a month. Therefore, it is multiplied by 12 to get the annual expenditure. This assumes that expenditure for the last month is representative of rest of the months in a year.

Estimation relies on assumptions relevant to each category. The same six categories, as in inpatient services, were used.

- Children
- Formal Sector
- Disabled
- Pensioners
- Others in State
- Everyone Else

The following questions from the survey and the Stata code were used for cleaning the data and generating the required variable for estimating the total outpatient expenditure by eligibility groups.

1. How much did you pay in total for medicines purchased during the past 30 days? (variable name: i1_20) Continuous variable which was used to derive out-of-pocket expenditures on drugs.
2. What is your employment status? (variable name: d1_5, see Table A1.5)

Table A1.5: Employment Status in the Integrated Living Conditions Survey (Discrete, Categorical Variable)

Value	Label
1	Employee with a written contract
2	Employee with a verbal agreement
3	Employer (owner with permanent employees)
4	Own-account worker in a farm
5	Other own-account worker
6	Unpaid family worker
7	Member of the producer, consumer cooperative

Source: World Bank. 2017. *Integrated Living Conditions Survey 2017.* https://microdata.worldbank.org/index.php/catalog/3591.

If value =1, respondent is assumed to be a member of the formal sector since there is a written contract of employment. Rest of the responses for this question are not utilized for defining any category.

3.   Are there any persons within the household who belong to any of the following social categories groups? (variable name: a2_1, a2_2, a2_3; see Table A1.6)

Table A1.6: Social Categories in the Integrated Living Conditions Survey (Discrete, Categorical Variable)

Value	Label
1	Disabled category 1
2	Disabled category 2
3	Disabled category 3
4	Disabled child under 18 years of age
5	Age
6	Privileged
7	For long service
8	Disabled
9	Loss of bread-winner pensioners
10	Partially
11	For old age
12	Disabled
13	Loss of bread-winner pensioners
14	For long service
15	Disabled
16	Loss of bread-winner pensioners
17	Child with one parent (under 21 years of age)
18	Single mother child (under 18 years of age)
19	Child of divorced parents (under 18 years of age)
20	Child without parents care (under 21 years of age)
21	Pregnant woman (12 and more weeks)
22	Student (under 23 years of age)
23	Unemployed
24	Unemployed, who has not more than 5 years to reach right of old-age pension
25	Single (childless) pensioner

Source: World Bank. 2017. *Integrated Living Conditions Survey 2017*. https://microdata.worldbank.org/index.php/catalog/3591.

If value = 1, 2, or 3, the respondent is classified as belonging to the disabled group.

If value = 4–25, the respondent is classified as belonging to Others in Social Order group.

Based on these questions, eligibility groups are formed according to:

- Group_dummy = 1 is the Children group: defined by including all those younger than 18 years in ILCS (solely based on age).
- Group_dummy = 2 is the Formal Sector group: defined by those who have a written employment contract and are between the ages of 17 and 64 years.
- Group_dummy = 3 is the Disabled group: defined by including all those who fall in disabled categories 1,2,3 and are between the ages of 17 and 64 years.
- Group_dummy = 4 is the Pensioners group: defined by including all those older than 63 years (solely based on age).
- Group_dummy = 5 is the State Order-Others group: these are left in social categories in ILCS and are between the ages of 17 and 64 years.
- Group_dummy = 6 is the Everyone Else group: This group includes all who are now left after defining all the above groups (do not have any social category and are between the ages of 17 and 64 years, and do not have a written employment contract).

The Stata code for deriving pharmaceutical expenditures is as follows:

```
**after opening the file 2016 ILCS members file**
gen group_dummy =.
replace group_dummy = 1 if age <18
**group_dummy==1 is the children eligibility group**
replace group_dummy = 2 if age>17 & age<64 & a2_1==. & d1_5==1
**group_dummy==2 is the formal sector**
replace group_dummy = 4 if age >63
**group_dummy==4 is the pensioners group**
replace group_dummy = 5 if age>17 & age<64 & a2_1!=. & a2_1>3
replace group_dummy = 5 if age>17 & age<64 & a2_2!=. & a2_2>3
replace group_dummy = 5 if age>17 & age<64 & a2_3!=. & a2_3>3
**group_dummy==5 is the state order others**
replace group_dummy = 3 if age>17 & age<64 & a2_1 == 1 | age>17 & age<64 & a2_1 == 2 |
age>17 & age<64 & a2_1 == 3
replace group_dummy = 3 if age>17 & age<64 & a2_2 == 1 | age>17 & age<64 & a2_2 == 2 |
age>17 & age<64 & a2_2 == 3
replace group_dummy = 3 if age>17 & age<64 & a2_3 == 1 | age>17 & age<64 & a2_3 == 2 |
age>17 & age<64 & a2_3 == 3
**group_dummy==3 is the disabled group**
replace group_dummy = 6 if age>17 & age<64 & group_dummy==.
**group_dummy==6 is the everyone else group**
gen pharma== i1_20 * 12
**pharma is i1_20 (outpatient drugs) annualized**
```

C.   Estimating the Unmet Need (Utilization Bump)

The utilization bump was estimated from the ILCS 2016. The survey asks questions regarding the utilization related to health services. Table A1.7 shows the questions that were used to estimate the total unmet need:

Table A1.7: If you did not seek medical advice during last 30 days, what was the reason why not?

Value	Response
1	Self-treatment
2	Could not afford treatment
3	Too far/ too difficult to reach
4	Problem wasn't serious enough
5	There was no need
6	Have doctor-relative or friend
7	Other

Source: World Bank. 2017. *Integrated Living Conditions Survey 2017*. https://microdata.worldbank.org/index.php/catalog/3591.

The following Stata code was used:

```
**after opening the ILCS 2016 members file**
collapse (sum) weight, by(i1_18)
egen tot = total(weight)
gen pct = (weight/tot)*100
browse
**this will open the data viewer and that will include the following estimated values**
```

Seventeen percent unmet demand was estimated (from rounding 16.8%).

The following options were included in unmet need:

- could not afford treatment (5.7)
- problem was not serious enough (9.2)
- have doctor-relative or friend (1.3)
- others (which mean that it was serious but person still did not visit) (0.6)

APPENDIX 2

Armenia Health Budget for 2020 and Projections for 2020–2022 According to the Medium-term Expenditure Framework (AMD '000): Indicative Amounts of State Budget Funding for 2020–2022

Budget Programs 2020			2020 Approved Budget 2021	Medium-Term Expenditure Framework 2020–2022		
				2020 (AMD)	2021 (AMD)	2022 (AMD)
No.	Index	Total State Budget Expenditures	1,855,697,119.5	1,871,676,695.7	2,027,746,008.6	2,235,466,753.9
		Ministry of Health	**109,324,584.9**	**107,213,297.7**	**115,287,257.7**	**126,350,331.5**
1.	1003	Protection of Public Health	5,772,875.6	5,744,584.9	5,914,008.3	5,914,008.3
2.	1053	Program for Modernization of Health System and Increasing Its Efficiency	3,038,874.3	3,102,399.1	3,306,213.9	–
3.	1099	Primary Health Care Services	27,058,857.7	25,866,757.7	27,907,184.7	27,907,184.7
4.	1126	Development of public policy for the healthcare sector, program coordination, and monitoring	991,878.8	1,036,704.3	3,522,496.5	13,152,148.2

continued on next page

Table continued

		Budget Programs 2020	2020 Approved Budget 2021	Medium-Term Expenditure Framework 2020–2022		
				2020 (AMD)	2021 (AMD)	2022 (AMD)
5.	1142	Forensic and pathoanatomical services	502,949.3	502,949.3	502,949.3	502,949.3
6.	1188	Provision of Medicine	3,265,171.1	3,250,799.4	3,451,177.1	3,451,177.1
7.	1191	Consulting, professional support, and studies	321,261.6	317,564.9	317,564.9	317,564.9
8.	1200	Protection of Maternal and Child Health	20,398,977.7	19,691,077.7	20,174,124.8	20,174,124.8
9.	1201	Medical ambulance service program	4,292,270.0	4,292,270.0	4,292,270.0	4,292,270.0
10.	1202	Providing medical care for noncommunicable diseases	13,707,535.6	13,650,839.6	15,932,309.6	15,932,309.6
11.	1207	Medical care of socially vulnerable people and those included in special categories	27,104,075.3	27,104,075.3	27,163,683.1	31,903,319.1
12.	1208	Infectious disease prevention program	2,869,857.9	2,653,275.5	2,803,275.5	2,803,275.5

— = not available.
Source: Republic of Armenia Medium-Term Expenditure Framework, 2020-2022, State Budget 2020.

Population Growth Rates

Table A3.1: Population Growth Rates for Children (Female), 2016–2021
(%)

Age Bracket (years)	2016	2017	2018	2019	2020	2021
[0–1]	(2.71)	(2.71)	(2.78)	(2.86)	(2.95)	(2.47)
[2–7]	(1.38)	(1.38)	(1.42)	(1.46)	(1.50)	(2.22)
[8–9]	(0.05)	(0.05)	(0.05)	(0.05)	(0.05)	(1.97)
[10–14]	2.99	2.99	2.91	2.82	2.75	0.73
[15–17]	(1.04)	(1.04)	(1.05)	(1.07)	(1.08)	3.09

( ) = negative.
Source: United Nations Department of Economic and Social Affairs. 2019. *World Population Prospects.* https://population.un.org/wpp/Download/Standard/Population/.

Table A3.2: Population Growth Rates for Children (Male), 2016–2021
(%)

Age Bracket (years)	2016	2017	2018	2019	2020	2021
[0–1]	(2.83)	(2.83)	(2.91)	(3.00)	(3.09)	(2.62)
[2–7]	(1.50)	(1.50)	(1.54)	(1.58)	(1.63)	(2.36)
[8–9]	(0.16)	(0.16)	(0.16)	(0.16)	(0.16)	(2.09)
[10–14]	2.81	2.81	2.73	2.66	2.59	0.53
[15–17]	(0.36)	(0.36)	(0.36)	(0.36)	(0.36)	2.76

( ) = negative.
Source: United Nations Department of Economic and Social Affairs. 2019. *World Population Prospects.* https://population.un.org/wpp/Download/Standard/Population/.

Table A3.3: Population Growth Rates for Formal Sector (Female), 2016–2021
(%)

Age Bracket (years)	2016	2017	2018	2019	2020	2021
[18–19]	(1.04)	(1.04)	(1.05)	(1.07)	(1.08)	3.09
[20–24]	(6.47)	(6.47)	(6.92)	(7.43)	(8.03)	(1.47)
[25–29]	(3.76)	(3.76)	(3.90)	(4.06)	(4.23)	(6.49)
[30–34]	1.13	1.13	1.11	1.10	1.09	(3.00)
[35–39]	3.99	3.99	3.83	3.69	3.56	1.77
[40–44]	2.18	2.18	2.13	2.09	2.05	4.52
[45–49]	(0.66)	(0.66)	(0.67)	(0.67)	(0.67)	3.01
[50–54]	(4.00)	(4.00)	(4.16)	(4.35)	(4.54)	(1.08)
[55–59]	(1.10)	(1.10)	(1.12)	(1.13)	(1.14)	(4.08)
[60–63]	5.93	5.93	5.60	5.30	5.03	(0.46)

( ) = negative.
Source: United Nations Department of Economic and Social Affairs. 2019. *World Population Prospects.* https://population.un.org/wpp/Download/Standard/Population/.

Table A3.4: Population Growth Rates for Formal Sector (Male), 2016–2021
(%)

Age Bracket (years)	2016	2017	2018	2019	2020	2021
[18–19]	(0.36)	(0.36)	(0.36)	(0.36)	(0.36)	2.76
[20–24]	(3.76)	(3.76)	(3.91)	(4.06)	(4.24)	(1.14)
[25–29]	(4.01)	(4.01)	(4.18)	(4.36)	(4.56)	(3.90)
[30–34]	0.62	0.62	0.61	0.61	0.61	(2.83)
[35–39]	1.84	1.84	1.81	1.77	1.74	2.84
[40–44]	1.17	1.17	1.16	1.14	1.13	4.35
[45–49]	(1.14)	(1.14)	(1.15)	(1.17)	(1.18)	3.04
[50–54]	(5.53)	(5.53)	(5.85)	(6.21)	(6.62)	(0.10)
[55–59]	(3.15)	(3.15)	(3.25)	(3.36)	(3.47)	(4.41)
[60–63]	4.73	4.73	4.52	4.32	4.14	(1.32)

( ) = negative.
Source: United Nations Department of Economic and Social Affairs. 2019. *World Population Prospects.* https://population.un.org/wpp/Download/Standard/Population/.

Table A3.5: Population Growth Rates for Disabled (Females), 2016–2021
(%)

Age Bracket (years)	2016	2017	2018	2019	2020	2021
[18–19]	(1.04)	(1.04)	(1.05)	(1.07)	(1.08)	3.09
[20–24]	(6.47)	(6.47)	(6.92)	(7.43)	(8.03)	(1.47)
[25–29]	(3.76)	(3.76)	(3.90)	(4.06)	(4.23)	(6.49)
[30–34]	1.13	1.13	1.11	1.10	1.09	(3.00)
[35–39]	3.99	3.99	3.83	3.69	3.56	1.77
[40–44]	2.18	2.18	2.13	2.09	2.05	4.52
[45–49]	(0.66)	(0.66)	(0.67)	(0.67)	(0.67)	3.01
[50–54]	(4.00)	(4.00)	(4.16)	(4.35)	(4.54)	(1.08)
[55–59]	(1.10)	(1.10)	(1.12)	(1.13)	(1.14)	(4.08)
[60–63]	5.93	5.93	5.60	5.30	5.03	(0.46)

( ) = negative.
Source: United Nations Department of Economic and Social Affairs. 2019. *World Population Prospects.* https://population.un.org/wpp/Download/Standard/Population/.

Table A3.6: Population Growth Rates for Disabled (Male), 2016–2021
(%)

Age Bracket (years)	2016	2017	2018	2019	2020	2021
[18–19]	(0.36)	(0.36)	(0.36)	(0.36)	(0.36)	2.76
[20–24]	(3.76)	(3.76)	(3.91)	(4.06)	(4.24)	(1.14)
[25–29]	(4.01)	(4.01)	(4.18)	(4.36)	(4.56)	(3.90)
[30–34]	0.62	0.62	0.61	0.61	0.61	(2.83)
[35–39]	1.84	1.84	1.81	1.77	1.74	2.84
[40–44]	1.17	1.17	1.16	1.14	1.13	4.35
[45–49]	(1.14)	(1.14)	(1.15)	(1.17)	(1.18)	3.04
[50–54]	(5.53)	(5.53)	(5.85)	(6.21)	(6.62)	(0.10)
[55–59]	(3.15)	(3.15)	(3.25)	(3.36)	(3.47)	(4.41)
[60 - 63]	4.73	4.73	4.52	4.32	4.14	(1.32)

( ) = negative.
Source: United Nations Department of Economic and Social Affairs. 2019. *World Population Prospects.* https://population.un.org/wpp/Download/Standard/Population/.

Table A3.7: Population Growth for Pensioners (Female), 2016–2021
(%)

Age Bracket (years)	2016	2017	2018	2019	2020	2021
[64–69]	4.56	4.56	4.37	4.18	4.01	5.87
[70–74]	11.77	11.77	10.53	9.53	8.70	7.15
[75+]	(3.02)	(3.02)	(3.11)	(3.21)	(3.32)	0.88

( ) = negative.
Source: United Nations Department of Economic and Social Affairs. 2019. *World Population Prospects.* https://population.un.org/wpp/Download/Standard/Population/.

Table A3.8: Population Growth Rates for Pensioners (Male), 2016–2021
(%)

Age Bracket (years)	2016	2017	2018	2019	2020	2021
[64–69]	4.34	4.34	4.16	4.00	3.84	5.19
[70–74]	12.23	12.23	10.90	9.83	8.95	6.77
[75+]	(4.25)	(4.25)	(4.43)	(4.64)	(4.87)	0.35

( ) = negative.
Source: United Nations Department of Economic and Social Affairs. 2019. *World Population Prospects.* https://population.un.org/wpp/Download/Standard/Population/.

Table A3.9: Population Growth Rates for Others in State Order (Female), 2016–2021
(%)

Age Bracket (years)	2016	2017	2018	2019	2020	2021
[18–19]	(1.04)	(1.04)	(1.05)	(1.07)	(1.08)	3.09
[20–24]	(6.47)	(6.47)	(6.92)	(7.43)	(8.03)	(1.47)
[25–29]	(3.76)	(3.76)	(3.90)	(4.06)	(4.23)	(6.49)
[30–34]	1.13	1.13	1.11	1.10	1.09	(3.00)
[35–39]	3.99	3.99	3.83	3.69	3.56	1.77
[40–44]	2.18	2.18	2.13	2.09	2.05	4.52
[45–49]	(0.66)	(0.66)	(0.67)	(0.67)	(0.67)	3.01
[50–54]	(4.00)	(4.00)	(4.16)	(4.35)	(4.54)	(1.08)
[55–59]	(1.10)	(1.10)	(1.12)	(1.13)	(1.14)	(4.08)
[60–63]	5.93	5.93	5.60	5.30	5.03	(0.46)

( ) = negative.
Source: United Nations Department of Economic and Social Affairs. 2019. *World Population Prospects.* https://population.un.org/wpp/Download/Standard/Population/.

Table A3.10: Population Growth Rates for Others in State Order (Male), 2016–2021
(%)

Age Bracket (years)	2016	2017	2018	2019	2020	2021
[18–19]	(0.36)	(0.36)	(0.36)	(0.36)	(0.36)	2.76)
[20–24]	(3.76)	(3.76)	(3.91)	(4.06)	(4.24)	(1.14)
[25–29]	(4.01)	(4.01)	(4.18)	(4.36)	(4.56)	(3.90)
[30–34]	0.62	0.62	0.61	0.61	0.61	(2.83)
[35–39]	1.84	1.84	1.81	1.77	1.74	2.84
[40–44]	1.17	1.17	1.16	1.14	1.13	4.35
[45–49]	(1.14)	(1.14)	(1.15)	(1.17)	(1.18)	3.04
[50–54]	(5.53)	(5.53)	(5.85)	(6.21)	(6.62)	(0.10)
[55–59]	(3.15)	(3.15)	(3.25)	(3.36)	(3.47)	(4.41)
[60–63]	4.73	4.73	4.52	4.32	4.14	(1.32)

( ) = negative.
Source: United Nations Department of Economic and Social Affairs. 2019. *World Population Prospects.* https://population.un.org/wpp/Download/Standard/Population/.

Table A3.11: Population Growth Rates for Everyone Else (Female), 2016–2021
(%)

Age Bracket (years)	2016	2017	2018	2019	2020	2021
[18–19]	(1.04)	(1.04)	(1.05)	(1.07)	(1.08)	3.09
[20–24]	(6.47)	(6.47)	(6.92)	(7.43)	(8.03)	(1.47)
[25–29]	(3.76)	(3.76)	(3.90)	(4.06)	(4.23)	(6.49)
[30–34]	1.13	1.13	1.11	1.10	1.09	(3.00)
[35–39]	3.99	3.99	3.83	3.69	3.56	1.77
[40–44]	2.18	2.18	2.13	2.09	2.05	4.52
[45–49]	(0.66)	(0.66)	(0.67)	(0.67)	(0.67)	3.01
[50–54]	(4.00)	(4.00)	(4.16)	(4.35)	(4.54)	(1.08)
[55–59]	(1.10)	(1.10)	(1.12)	(1.13)	(1.14)	(4.08)
[60–63]	5.93	5.93	5.60	5.30	5.03	(0.46)

( ) = negative.
Source: United Nations Department of Economic and Social Affairs. 2019. *World Population Prospects.* https://population.un.org/wpp/Download/Standard/Population/.

Table A3.12: Population Growth Rates for Everyone Else (Male), 2016–2021
(%)

Age Bracket (years)	2016	2017	2018	2019	2020	2021
[18–19]	(0.36)	(0.36)	(0.36)	(0.36)	(0.36)	2.76
[20–24]	(3.76)	(3.76)	(3.91)	(4.06)	(4.24)	(1.14)
[25–29]	(4.01)	(4.01)	(4.18)	(4.36)	(4.56)	(3.90)
[30–34]	0.62	0.62	0.61	0.61	0.61	(2.83)
[35–39]	1.84	1.84	1.81	1.77	1.74	2.84
[40–44]	1.17	1.17	1.16	1.14	1.13	4.35
[45–49]	(1.14)	(1.14)	(1.15)	(1.17)	(1.18)	3.04%
[50–54]	(5.53)	(5.53)	(5.85)	(6.21)	(6.62)	(0.10)
[55–59]	(3.15)	(3.15)	(3.25)	(3.36)	(3.47)	(4.41)
[60–63]	4.73	4.73	4.52	4.32	4.14	(1.32)

( ) = negative.
Source: United Nations Department of Economic and Social Affairs. 2019. *World Population Prospects.* https://population.un.org/wpp/Download/Standard/Population/.

Mapping of the Ministry of Health Budget to Eligibility Groups

Mapping with the Ministry of Health Budget	Eligibility Groups	People Eligible in 2016 (No.)	Actual Expense—Baseline (AMD '000)
Expenditures for programs already available to all Armenians, regardless of social status:			
PHC, Outpatient, Emergency Care, Vertical Programs of Hospital Care	—	—	**33,050,849.81**
PHC	All Armenians	2,997,974	10,906,441.61
Sports medicine and anti-doping control services	All Armenians	2,997,974	101,735.10
HIV/AIDS prevention and care services	All Armenians	2,997,974	284,903.80
Narrow specialized medical services (PHC level)	All Armenians	2,997,974	3,978,248.33
Medical services for diseases requiring continuous control and separate diseases	All Armenians	2,997,974	132,997.90
Emergency medical services for outpatient (Medical Ambulance Services)	All Armenians	2,997,974	3,241,597.10
Laboratory (PHC level)	All Armenians	2,997,974	3,237,456.18
Emergency medical services for hospital services	All Armenians	2,997,974	1,997,650.40
Medical care services during emergency situations	All Armenians	2,997,974	10,714.40
Tuberculosis medical care services	All Armenians	2,997,974	1,405,028.57

continued on next page

Table *continued*

Mapping with the Ministry of Health Budget	Eligibility Groups	People Eligible in 2016 (No.)	Actual Expense—Baseline (AMD '000)
Tuberculosis, maternal and child health and family planning/reproductive health outcomes in Armenia grant program	All Armenians	2,997,974	601,907.60
Global fund-supported grant program on strengthening the prevention of the tuberculosis in Armenia	All Armenians	2,997,974	1,064,057.01
Global fund-supported grant program on assisting National HIV/AIDS program in Armenia	All Armenians	2,997,974	402,370.57
Medical care services for intestinal and other infectious diseases	All Armenians	2,997,974	1,218,621.63
Medical care services for sexually transmitted diseases	All Armenians	2,997,974	181,344.10
Medical care services for patients with drug and mental health disorders	All Armenians	2,997,974	2,703,736.55
Medical care services of oncology and hematology diseases	All Armenians	2,997,974	1,139,028.26
Forensic and genetic services	All Armenians	2,997,974	389,846.00
Pathogenic services	All Armenians	2,997,974	53,164.70
Public Health (Children)	—	697,528	-
Public Health (All Other Groups)	—	2,997,974	**4,861,241.67**
National immunization program service support grant	All Armenians	2,997,974	13,694.80
Hygienic and epidemiological expertise services	All Armenians	2,997,974	105,213.99
Services for the disinfection of infectious diseases centers	All Armenians	2,997,974	75,017.10
Blood collection services	All Armenians	2,997,974	252,758.10
National Immunization Program	All Armenians	2,997,974	1,440,378.83
Services ensuring the sanitary and epidemiological safety of the population and public health services	All Armenians	2,997,974	2,878,696.80
Promotion of healthy lifestyles and public awareness-raising services	All Armenians	2,997,974	87,682.05
Healthy nutrition for children public awareness services	Children	697,528	7,800.00
Catastrophic and Other individual Programs (Based on a Mix of Social Vulnerability and Medical Condition Criteria)	—	—	**5,735,756.15**

continued on next page

Table *continued*

Mapping with the Ministry of Health Budget	Eligibility Groups	People Eligible in 2016 (No.)	Actual Expense—Baseline (AMD '000)
Hemodialysis services	All Armenians	2,997,974	2,069,048.80
Heart Surgery Services	All Armenians	2,997,974	3,615,925.30
Medical services with reproductive auxiliary technologies for infertile couples	All Armenians	2,997,974	35,836.60
Compensation of the travel cost of the patients referred to abroad for the treatment	All Armenians	2,997,974	14,945.45
Women's Programs	—	1,032,000	**8,653,086.77**
Obstetric medical care services	Women of reproductive age	1,032,000	6,720,279.02
Gynecological diseases medical care services (hospital)	Women of reproductive age	1,032,000	354,513.98
Gynecological medical assistance (outpatient)	Women of reproductive age	1,032,000	1,532,473.77
Ensure accessibility to modern mean of contraceptives to prevent unwanted pregnancies	Women of reproductive age	1,032,000	45,820.00
Expenditures for Programs Only Available to Special Groups	—	—	**2,662,817.80**
Dental care for children	Children (6 and 12 years old only)	75,782	77,259.20
Examination and medical service for military and pre-military individuals: paramedical (PHC level)	Children (young males 14–17 years old)	74,631	566,313.40
Provision of the orthoses and corsets to disabled and needy children	Children (disabled)	8,047	81,811.00
Dental care	Children, Pensioners, Socially Vulnerable	1,013,536	748,246.30
	Children 0–7 years old	329,284	—
	Disabled	131,674	—
	State Order—Others	188,312	—
	Pensioner	364,266	—
Rehabilitation medical care services	Certain Diagnosis and Socially Vulnerable	319,986	610,473.90
	Disabled	131,674	—
	State Order—Others	188,312	—

continued on next page

Table *continued*

Mapping with the Ministry of Health Budget	Eligibility Groups	People Eligible in 2016 (No.)	Actual Expense—Baseline (AMD '000)
Expensive diagnostic examination	Vulnerable and Special Groups	319,986	578,714.00
	Disabled	131,674	—
	State Order—Others	188,312	—
Administration, capital expenditure and others	—	2,997,974	**9,727,340.47**
Replenishment of the medical equipment for hospitals and medical station	—	—	10,147.07
Expertise and methodological services derived from pharmacy policy	—	—	20,757.80
Construction of health facilities	—	—	894,430.30
Consulting, research and specialized support medical care	—	—	225,223.00
Purchase, customs clearance and distribution services of medicines and pharmaceutical products for humanitarian aid	—	—	59,711.34
Provision of the medical services in the regional health organizations through temporarily referrals of the medical professionals	—	—	5,332.45
Additional financing program for Health System Modernization Second Project supported by the World Bank	—	—	45,249.79
Noncommunicable disease prevention and control program supported by the World Bank	—	—	6,223,794.55
Supported by United States Center for Disease Control and Prevention	—	—	95,499.03
Noncommunicable disease prevention and control grant project supported by the World Bank	—	—	209,497.79
Elaboration of the financial project based on performance of the disease prevention and control grant project support by the World Bank	—	—	8,511.61
Doctors' trips to examine the experiences of foreign leading clinics	—	—	21,121.07
Coordination of the National tuberculosis prevention program	—	—	62,060.90

continued on next page

Table *continued*

Mapping with the Ministry of Health Budget	Eligibility Groups	People Eligible in 2016 (No.)	Actual Expense—Baseline (AMD '000)
Maintenance and operation of medical equipment of the hospital and health centers	—	—	28,591.00
Maintenance of the executive power, state and territorial governance bodies (for the ministerial staff)			1,817,412.77
Total for services not for expansion	—	—	**64,691,092.67**
Expenditures only for selected groups, targeted for expansion			
Inpatient (and some outpatient)	—	—	—
Medical services for socially vulnerable and special groups	Disabled and State Order—others	368,404	6,378,501.44
	Disabled	131,674	2,817,823.60
	Pensioners	48,418	1,563,901.40
	State Order—Others	188,312	2,050,529.37
Medical care services to military service personnel as well as rescue workers and their family members	Formal (military)	—	2,354,124.40
Medical care and service for employees of the state institutions and organizations	Formal (civil servants)	—	2,644,436.89
Hospital medical care services and examination for military and pre-military individuals	Formal (military)	—	845,942.17
Medical care service for victims of trafficking	State Order—Others	—	—
Children's medical care services	Children	—	8,142,551.96
Pharmaceuticals			
Provision of Medicine to individuals receiving outpatient, hospital care, and individuals included in special groups	Disabled, children, other social groups	649,270	3,329,241.14
	Disabled	131,674	—
	Children aged 0–7 years	329,284	—
	State Order—Others	188,312	—
Provision of the medicine to state security service	Military	215,313	1,115.10
Total for expansion	—	—	**23,695,913.10**
Total expenditure for 2016	—	—	**88,387,005.77**

"—": not available or not applicable.
PHC = primary health care.
Source: Ministry of Finance.

References

M. Goldburd et al. 2016. *Generalized Linear Models for Insurance Rating*. Casualty Actuarial Society. https://www.casact.org/pubs/monographs/papers/05-Goldburd-Khare-Tevet.pdf.

Y. Guerard et al. 2011. *Actuarial Costing of Universal Health Insurance Coverage in Indonesia: Options and Preliminary Results (English)*. Washington, DC: World Bank. http://documents.worldbank.org/curated/en/685921468039053176/Actuarial-costing-of-universal-health-insurance-coverage-in-Indonesia-options-and-preliminary-results.

International Monetary Fund (IMF). 2019. Republic of Armenia: 2019 Article IV Consultation and Request for a Stand-By Arrangement-Press Release; Staff Report; and Statement by the Executive Director for the Republic of Armenia. *IMF Country Report*. No. 19/154. Washington, DC. https://www.imf.org/en/Publications/CR/Issues/2019/06/05/Republic-of-Armenia-2019-Article-IV-Consultation-and-Request-for-a-Stand-By-Arrangement-46968.

———. 2020. World Economic Outlook Databases. https://www.imf.org/en/Publications/SPROLLs/world-economic-outlook-databases#sort=%40imfdate%20descending.

M. Jowett. 2016. *Why Does UHC Performance Vary So Much Across Countries, At Any Given Level of Health Spending?* PowerPoint presentation prepared for GIZ Symposium, Retreat on Health, Social Protection and Inclusion. Germany. 8 September.http://health.bmz.de/events/Events_2015/A_Retreat_on_Health__Social_Protection_and_Inclusion_2016/06_breakout_1_5/Jowett_break_out_session_8_Sept_2016.pdf.

R. Lavado, S. Hayrapetyan, and S. Kharazyan. 2018. Expansion of the Benefit Package: The Experience of Armenia. *Universal Health Care Coverage Series*. No 27. Washington, DC: World Bank Group.

J. Mawejje and R. K. Sebudde. 2019. Tax Revenue Potential and Effort: Worldwide Estimates Using a New Dataset. *Economic Analysis and Policy*. 63(C). pp. 119–129.

National Institute of Health. 2020. *2019 National Health Accounts*. Yerevan. http://nih.am/assets/pdf/atvk/3a71b247c965d4cce6002a3229447583.pdf

E. Ohlsson and B. Johansson. 2010. *Non-Life Insurance Pricing with Generalized Linear Models*. Berlin Heidelberg: Springer-Verlag.

E. Richardson. 2013. Armenia: Health System Review. *Health Systems in Transition*. 15(4). pp.1–99.

Statistical Committee of the Republic of Armenia. 2018. *Social Snapshot and Poverty in Armenia, 2008-2017*. https://www.armstat.am/file/article/poverty_2018_english_2.pdf.

M. Tadevosyan et al. 2019. Factors Contributing to Rapidly Increasing Caesarian Section in Armenia: A Partially Mixed Concurrent Quantitative-Qualitative Equal Status Study. *BMC Pregnancy and Childbirth*. 19 (2). https://bmcpregnancychildbirth.biomedcentral.com/articles/10.1186/s12884-018-2158-6.

UNSTAT. 2020. Demographic Statistics Database. http://data.un.org/Data.aspx?d=POP&f=tableCode%3A2.

World Bank. 2020. World Development Indicators. https://datacatalog.worldbank.org/dataset/world-development-indicators.

World Health Organization. 2020. Global Health Expenditure Database. https://apps.who.int/nha/database/Select/Indicators/en.